CLUE

CLUE

A GUIDE THROUGH GREEK TO HEBREW SCRIPTURE

BY

EDWIN A. ABBOTT

'Ἀποδείξεως δ' οὔσης ἀνάγκη συγκαταβαίνειν εἰς τὰς ζητήσεις, 'If there is such a thing as demonstration people must condescend to investigate.'—Clem. Alex. *Miscellanies*, vii. 15.

PUBLISHERS
Eugene, Oregon

Wipf and Stock Publishers
199 W 8th Ave, Suite 3
Eugene, OR 97401

Clue
A Guide through Greek to Hebrew Scripture
By Abbott, Edwin A.
ISBN: 1-59752-162-0
Publication date 4/25/2005
Previously published by Adam and Charles Black, 1900

TO
TROMMIUS AND BRUDER
AND THE WHOLE OF THE UNKNOWN ARMY
OF PATIENT PLODDERS
THIS BOOK IS DEDICATED
BY ONE OF THEM

PREFACE

THIS book, called *Clue* for brief reference, is the First Part of a series (to be entitled *Diatessarica*) dealing with the interpretation of the Gospels.

Part I.—which is of a more popular character than the rest, and requires from the reader no knowledge of Greek or Hebrew—aims at demonstrating that portions of the Synoptic Gospels are translated, or modified by translation, from Hebrew documents.

Part II., which will be published almost simultaneously with Part I., aims at demonstrating that Mark contains a tradition from which Matthew and Luke borrowed, and discusses the corrections of Mark adopted jointly by Matthew and Luke.

Part III. will contain the whole of the text of Mark, with such parts of the other Gospels as are parallel to Mark. The text will be divided into small passages, each accompanied by its commentary. This, being for the most part the common tradition of the first three Gospels, may conveniently be called the Triple Tradition.

Part IV.—not yet in writing—will contain what may conveniently be called the Double Tradition, *i.e.*

passages not found in Mark but only in Matthew and Luke.

Part V. will contain John.

Part VI. will contain the Gospel of the Resurrection as given by the Mark-Appendix, Matthew, Luke, and John.

Part VII.—not yet in writing—will contain Single Traditions, *i.e.* portions peculiar to Matthew, and to Luke, including the account of Christ's birth.

Before Part VIII. can be described, a little explanation is needed. It is maintained by the author that parts of the first three Gospels are derived from a Hebrew original (which has also influenced the fourth). Now in the Greek Old Testament we find a multitude of errors arising from the inability of the translators to distinguish Hebrew letters, and to understand Hebrew words and idioms. In the Synoptic Gospels of the Greek New Testament, then, we may expect (on our hypothesis) to find the same errors, fewer, of course, but still the same in kind. For example, a constant source of error in the Greek Old Testament is the similarity between the Hebrew letters d and r (ד and ר), so that (to take one instance) "Edom" (אדם) and "Aram" (ארם) are repeatedly confused by the translators, who give us "Idumaea" for "Syria," or *vice versa*.

The object of Part VIII. is to tabulate, in their Greek alphabetical order, errors of this kind found in the Greek Old Testament, with the view of detecting similar errors—if any such exist—in the Greek New Testament. For example, the error above mentioned

PREFACE

would be tabulated not under the Hebrew names of "Edom" and "Aram," but under their Greek equivalents "Idumaea" and "Syria." Then, if we should find in one of the Synoptic Gospels an unexpected mention of "Idumaea," our tabulated lists would suggest to us that—instead of trying to find historical reasons (where none appear to exist) for a statement about Idumaea—the right course is to look first in the parallel Gospels for some mention of Syria. If "Syria" is there, we shall conclude that the discrepancy arises from translating a Hebrew original. Then will begin the task—in some cases a far more difficult task—of deciding which of the two readings is correct.

For the construction of such a Key, some materials are available from the invaluable Concordance to the Septuagint compiled by Trommius—to whom, in company with Bruder, the compiler of the New Testament Concordance, this work is dedicated. But Trommius has left a great many explicable errors unexplained. Moreover, it did not lie within the province of Trommius to set side by side parallel Hebrew books or parallel versions of the same Hebrew book, and to classify the variations in Greek resulting sometimes from the variations of two Hebrew sources, sometimes from the divergent interpretations of one Hebrew text by two translators. All this then remains to be done.

As regards parallel versions, the author has tabulated the divergences in the two versions of Daniel, in Ezra compared with the First Book of Esdras, and in large portions of the Books of Samuel and Kings compared with Chronicles (or, in some cases, with the Psalms and Isaiah). But it has not been found possible as yet to tabulate all the verbal errors scattered through the pages of the Septuagint, nor can the author hope ever to achieve this task. It is the business of a University, not of a single student, and one of the objects of this Preface is to suggest to the Universities of Europe and America that such a work would be well worthy of them. To be complete, it should not be confined to mere words, but should contain Greek errors classified under other heads, such as, Person, Mood, Voice, Insertion, Omission, Interrogative, Negative, Subject, Metaphor reduced to Prose, Speech converted to Narrative, etc.

The author's approximation to this object, if published in his lifetime, will follow the seven Parts above mentioned. It is daily growing and, as he believes, daily becoming more useful. If published, it would be a more complete and less popular form of *Clue*, and might be entitled *Filum Labyrinthi*.

Obligations must be acknowledged to many friends for the revision of the proofs of this work; and, in particular, to the Rev. C. Taylor, D.D., Master of St. John's College, Cambridge, the Rev. W. H. Bennett, M.A., Professor of Old Testament Languages and Literature at Hackney and New Colleges, London, and Mr. W. S. Aldis, M.A., formerly Principal of the Durham College of Science, Newcastle-on-Tyne, for corrections and suggestions on points of Hebrew.

    WELLSIDE
    HAMPSTEAD
    9/9/1900

CONTENTS

REFERENCES AND ABBREVIATIONS . . . . Page xv

INTRODUCTION xvii

BOOK I

THE SEPTUAGINT

CHAPTER I

SPECIMENS OF ERROR IN THE SEPTUAGINT

§ 1. On the evidence needed to prove translation. § 2. On the evidence obtainable to prove translation from Hebrew into Greek. § 3. Specimens of Greek error arising from confusion of similar Hebrew letters. § 4. Specimens of Greek error arising from confusion of similar Hebrew words. § 5. The place of Christ's baptism : Bethabara? Betharaba? or Bethany? § 6. On the evidence required to prove translation from Hebrew in the Synoptic Gospels . . . . Page 3

CHAPTER II

THE ERROR OF CONFLATION

§ 1. Conflations, their nature and origin. § 2. Conflations, mostly caused by obscurity. § 3. Rules for returning through a conflation to the Original. § 4. Conflation mostly the sign of an early translation . . 19

CLUE

CHAPTER III

CONFLATIONS OF NAMES

* (see p. xix. n.) § 1. Specimens of name conflation. * § 2. "Darius." § 3. Luke's misunderstanding about Herod Antipas. § 4. "The son of Timaeus, Bartimaeus"; the development of different accounts about the person. or persons, denoted in the story of " Bartimaeus " . . . Page 27

CHAPTER IV

CONFLATIONS OF TECHNICAL TERMS, DATES, ETC.

§ 1. Technical terms. § 2. Conflations of dates. § 3. The hour of the Crucifixion 46

CHAPTER V

OTHER TYPICAL CONFLATIONS

* § 1. Variations of grammatical form. * § 2. Longer conflations. § 3. Hebrew conflations. § 4. Prejudice a cause of error. § 5. The "four sons" of Araunah 53

CHAPTER VI

CONFLATIVE VERSIONS

§ 1. The First Book of Esdras. § 2. The Septuagint Version of Daniel (parts of this are marked *). § 3. Conflations arising from Aramaic . . 67

BOOK II

THE SYNOPTIC GOSPELS

CHAPTER I

SPECIMENS OF CONFLATION

§ 1. (Mark i. 28) "The surrounding country of Galilee." § 2. (Mark i. 32, lit.) "It having become late, when the sun had set." § 3. (Mark iv. 5, 6, lit.)

CONTENTS

"It (*i.e.* the seed) arose . . . there arose the sun." § 4. (Mark iv. 40) "Why are ye fearful? Have ye not yet faith?" § 5. (Luke viii. 25, lit.) "Fearing they wondered." Conflated? § 6. (Luke ix. 37) "On the next day . . . from the mountain" . . . . Page 79

CHAPTER II

CONFLATIONS IN THE STORY OF THE GADARENE

§ 1. Conflative tendency apparent in Mark. § 2. (Mark v. 10) "the country"; (Luke viii. 31) "the abyss" 89

CHAPTER III

CONFUSIONS OF WORDS

§ 1. (Mark iii. 8) "Idumaea"; (Matthew iv. 24) "Syria." § 2. The prophecy of Amos concerning "Edom." § 3. (Matthew v. 48; xix. 21) "perfect" (i) (Mark x. 21, and Luke xviii. 22) "lacking" or "wanting." (ii.) (Luke vi. 36) "compassionate." § 4. (Mark vi. 33; Matthew xiv. 13) "on foot," an error. § 5. (Mark vi. 32; Matthew xiv. 13) "in the (or, a) boat to a desert place"; (Luke ix. 10) "to a city called Bethsaida." § 6. Was "boat" in the original? § 7. The "earthquake" recorded by Matthew (xxvii. 54) alone. § 8. Peter "sitting" or "standing" during the three denials? § 9. Peter (Mark xiv. 54) "warming himself" at the light [? of a fire]. § 10. (Mark iv. 21) "come"; (Matthew v. 15) "light"; (Luke viii. 16) "kindle." § 11. Matthew's use of "Companion!" § 12. (Mark i. 13) "wild beasts"; (Matthew iv. 2; Luke iv. 2) "he hungered." § 13. The healing of the "paralytic": (Mark ii. 3) "by four"; (Matthew ix. 2, Luke v. 18) "on a bed." § 14. The healing of the paralytic: origin of Mark's details. § 15. (Mark ii. 23) "making a way"; (Luke vi. 1) "rubbing with their hands" 97

CHAPTER IV

CONFUSIONS OF IDIOM

§ 1. (Mark xiv. 30) "Before the cock crow twice thrice . . . ." § 2. (Mark xiv. 1, Matthew xxvi. 2) "After two days"; (Luke xxii. 1) "drawing nigh." § 3. (Matthew x. 29) "two for a farthing"; (Luke xii. 6) "five for two farthings." § 4. (Mark viii. 31) "after three days"; (Matthew xvi. 21, and Luke ix. 22) "on the third day." § 5. (Matthew xviii. 22) "seventy times seven"; (Luke xvii. 4) "seven times turn." § 6. On the error that led

xiii

Luke to suppose that there were "other seventy [two] disciples." § 7. Errors arising from the Hebrew "and." § 8. Indicative confused with non-indicative forms. § 9. (Mark iv. 36) "they receive him"; (Matthew viii. 23, Luke viii. 22) "he went." § 10. Mark (iv. 36) alone mentions "other boats." § 11. (Matthew x. 28) "destroying"; (Luke xii. 5) "casting." § 12. (Matthew x. 29) "fall to the ground without"; (Luke xii. 6) "forgotten in the sight of." § 13. (Matthew v. 47) "salute"; (Luke vi. 33) "do good to." § 14. (Luke v. 20) "Man, thy sins are forgiven thee." § 15. (Mark vi. 8) "nothing . . . except a staff"; (Matthew x. 10) "nor a staff"; (Luke ix. 3) "neither a staff." § 16. (Mark ix. 41) lit. "in the Name because ye are Christ's." § 17. Hebraic alternatives. § 18. Conclusion . . . . Page 128

REFERENCES

(i.) *Black Arabic numbers*, e.g. (**27**), refer to subsections in this volume, or (if exceeding **272**) to subsections in Part II. ; (**27a**) means a footnote on subsection **27**.

(ii.) The books of Scripture are referred to by the ordinary abbreviations, except where specified below. But when it is said that Samuel, Isaiah, Matthew, or any other writer, wrote this or that, it is to be understood as meaning *the writer, whoever he may be, of the words in question*, and not as meaning that the actual writer was Samuel, Isaiah, or Matthew.

(iii.) In the notes, the MSS. known severally as the Alexandrian, the Sinaitic, the Vatican, and the Codex Bezae, are called by their usual abbreviations A, א, B, and D. The Syriac version of the Gospels discovered by Mrs. Gibson on Mount Sinai is called in the text the "Syro-Sinaitic" or "Sinaitic Syrian," and in the notes is referred to as SS.

(iv.) The text of the Greek Old Testament adopted is that of Professor Swete[1]; of the New, that of Westcott and Hort.

ABBREVIATIONS

A and א. *See* (iii.) above.
B. *See* (iii.) above.
Chr. = *Chronicles*.
D. *See* (iii.) above.
Ency. = Black's *Encyclopædia Biblica*.
Esdras, the First Book of, is frequently called, in the text, Esdras.

[1] This differs greatly from that of most earlier editions, which are usually based on Codex A. (**33**).

CLUE

Hor. Heb. = *Horae Hebraicae*, by John Lightfoot, 1658-74, ed. Gandell, Oxf. 1859.
K. = *Kings*.
leg. = (as in Tromm.) "legerunt," *i.e.* the LXX "read" so-and-so instead of the present Hebrew text.
Oxf. Conc. = *The Oxford Concordance to the Septuagint.*
S. = *Samuel.*
Schöttg. = Schöttgen's *Horae Hebraicae*, 1733.
Sir. = the work of the son of Sirach, commonly called Ecclesiasticus (see 20*a*).
SS. *See* (iii.) above.
Tisch. = Tischendorf's New Testament.
Tromm. = Trommius' *Concordance to the Septuagint.*
Wetst. = Wetstein's *Commentary on the New Testament*, 1751.
W. H. = Westcott and Hort's New Testament.

(*a*) A bracketed Arabic number, following the sign =, and intervening between a Hebrew and a Greek word, indicates the number of instances in which that Hebrew word is represented by that Greek word in the LXX—*e.g.* יצת = (7) ἀνάπτειν.

(*b*) * For the meaning of the asterisk prefixed to the headings of some sections, see p. xix n.

(*c*) In cases where the verses of the Hebrew, the Greek, and the Revised Version are numbered differently, the numbering of the Revised Version is for the most part given alone.

INTRODUCTION

THE primary object of this work is to indicate means for constructing a clue by which scholars may systematically find their way through any Greek translation from Hebrew back to the Hebrew original.

The secondary object is to demonstrate that parts of the Synoptic Gospels are based upon a common original Hebrew document, not Aramaic, but Hebrew in the strict sense, biblical Hebrew.[1]

Another object is to give specimens of the manner in which one may employ the clue so as to return from the Gospels to their original Hebrew.

Some years ago, the notion that a Jewish Christian

---

[1] See *Encyclopædia Biblica*, vol. i. col. 283 : "By the time of Christ Aramaic had long been the current popular speech of the Jews in Palestine, and the use, spoken and written, of Hebrew (in a greatly modified form) was confined to scholars. Christ and the apostles spoke Aramaic, and the original preaching of Christianity, the Εὐαγγέλιον, was in the same language. And this, too, not in the dialect current in Jerusalem, which roughly coincided with the literary language of the period, but in that of Galilee." Professor Nöldeke, the writer of the above, adds, "it is impossible for us to know the Galilean dialect of that period with accuracy. The attempts made in our days to reduce the words of Jesus from Greek to their original language have therefore failed."

By "the original preaching" Professor Nöldeke presumably means the oral Gospel preached during and after Christ's lifetime in Palestine.

It is quite possible that in the written Hebrew Gospel, Aramaic words were included (as in Ecclesiastes), and even Aramaic passages (as in Ezra and Daniel).

would write a Gospel in Hebrew, a dead language, might have been dismissed by many as absurd. But the recent discovery of the lost Hebrew of portions of Ecclesiasticus [1] reveals a Jew, long after Hebrew had ceased to be spoken, writing with fair success in "biblical Hebrew," just as the chroniclers of the life of St. Francis might write the Saint's words (as well as his deeds) in Latin, though St. Francis spoke in Italian. This in itself—apart from the opinion of so learned and laborious a scholar as Professor Resch—ought to convince people that there is no antecedent improbability in the hypothesis that the earliest written Gospel was composed in biblical Hebrew.

From this original Hebrew to ascend still further to the Galilaean Aramaic actually uttered by our Lord, is a different object—possibly attainable, and certainly not under-rated by the author, but not contemplated in this treatise. On the hypothesis of a Hebrew Gospel, the differences between Aramaic and Hebrew will not be likely to affect that large portion of the Gospels in which the evangelists, speaking in their own person, describe Christ's birth, death, resurrection, and miracles.

The earliest Christian ecclesiastical historian, Papias, tells us that "Matthew composed the *Logia* in the Hebrew language, and each one interpreted them as he could." [2] This external evidence dissipates a good deal of the alleged improbability of a Hebrew original. However, neither external evidence nor antecedent probabilities will find much space in the following pages. For it is there maintained that the internal evidence derivable from a Greek document can as absolutely and scientifically demonstrate translation from biblical Hebrew documents,[3] as fossils in a rock can demon-

---
[1] See below **20**a.
[2] Quoted by Eusebius in his *History of the Church*, iii. 39, 30.
[3] "Documents," not "document." The Hebrew *Logia* would be "interpreted" differently by Hebrew editors as well as by Greek translators. Some

INTRODUCTION

strate the action of water. The details of the demonstration will be often necessarily technical, but its fundamental principles can be made clear to the simplest intelligence. And even of the details a large number can be mastered without knowledge of any ancient language.[1] For the scholar, the statements made in the text will be demonstrated by quotations from the Hebrew Bible and from the Greek translations of it. These the "unlearned" reader will be unable to understand. Similarly, in a Court of Justice, a juror may be unable to understand the words of a foreign witness. He depends on the interpreter. But he is not thereby excluded from giving a verdict, and his verdict is generally right.

This is as it should be. It seems intolerable that, on points vitally affecting the religion and spiritual development of the multitudes, the ultimate judgment should rest with a few linguistic or theological specialists. The truth is—and to show that it is true is another object of this work—that what is called "the higher criticism" is simply scientific investigation and classification submitted to the judgment of common sense.

parts of Ecclesiasticus are rewritten in the margin by the Hebrew editor. Oral teaching would also produce variations. Hence the original Hebrew "document" would soon become "documents," perhaps intermixed with Aramaic words (see 126).

[1] For the purposes of reference and demonstration it has been necessary, in some sections, to accumulate instances of Septuagint error more numerous and more difficult than would be needed for mere illustration. Such sections are indicated by an asterisk, and the general reader is recommended to pass over them at first, returning to them when they are referred to in the later pages that deal with the Synoptic Gospels.

BOOK I
THE SEPTUAGINT

CHAPTER I

SPECIMENS OF ERROR IN THE SEPTUAGINT

§ 1. *On the evidence needed to prove translation*

[1] SUPPOSE we are reading two English histories of the French Revolution and find them so closely agreeing as to suggest that the two were borrowed from a common source. Comparing two corresponding sentences, we find, let us say, in one, "I assure you I *am* your friend in this affair," but in the other "I assure you I *follow* your friend in this affair." Ought we not at once to suspect—if we know anything of French—that this difference arises from translating into English the ambiguous French "suis"? Again, a page or two afterwards, we find in one of the histories (let us suppose) "he *was in good health*," but in the parallel portion of the other "he *was carrying his goods*." Surely this should suggest that "il portait ses biens" has been mistaken for the more familiar "il se portait bien"; and the result will be to strengthen our impression that parts of the two histories consist of translations made from one and the same French document. If, a little later, we met with two such parallels as "he *found for himself* in the town a young artist," and, "*there happened to be* in the town a young artist," our strong impression would be exchanged for an absolute conviction that these three errors were to be explained by one cause, translation from French. The original was, in the last case, "il se trouvait."

[2] Now take a case where there are no parallel documents and where the history is in a dead language. Suppose a Byzantine historian to be describing in Greek the invasion of Italy by the Goths. We know nothing of Greek; but, reading his work in a faithful English translation, we are perplexed by finding that the historian mentions "oaks" where we should have expected "flint-stones" or "flinty rocks"; and on the next page he has "the waters of *all* Italy" where "the waters of *a river* of Italy" would be much more to the point, and where "*all* Italy" is absurd. Turning to the annotations we are informed that "ilices" is the Latin for "oaks," and "silices" for "flint-stones"; and again that "omnis Italiae" is the Latin for "*of all* Italy," and "*amnis* Italiae" for "*a river* of Italy." We know nothing of Latin, and nothing of Greek; but if our annotator brought forward two or three more of such errors, and assured us that none of them could be explained as Greek misprints, should we feel any hesitation in accepting his statement—though based entirely on internal evidence—that these errors arose from mistranslated Latin? "What do you know about Greek or Latin?" some one might say to us. "Nothing," we should reply, "but we know something about the laws of evidence, and we have some claim to common sense."

§ 2. *On the evidence obtainable to prove translation from Hebrew into Greek*

From the preceding instances it appears that if we desired to ascertain whether an English document was translated from a French one, it would be well to make a list of such English words as were found by experience to be associated with errors in translating from the latter language, *e.g.* "follow" and "am," "find" and "happen to be," "carry" and "be in [good] health," etc. We should then be on our guard whenever we met such words in an English passage that seemed to contain a misstatement, and might be able, by means of our tabulated list or key, to restore the original French and rectify the error.

In the case of French, it would be a matter of great difficulty to compose a Key that would be of any practical service. The language is too well known, and modern criticism is too exacting, to allow English translations of French works to be published with many errors, or, if published, to remain in circulation. But in the case of Hebrew, things are widely different.

[3] The Greek Version of the Old Testament, called the Version of the Seventy, or the Septuagint—from the supposed number of the translators—teems with mistranslations arising from confusions between similar Hebrew letters, from the ambiguity of Hebrew forms, and from a general obscurity in Hebrew syntax owing to its inadequate supply of moods and conjunctions. Hence, it is easy to find materials for a Greek-Hebrew Key such as has been suggested above. The difficulty here consists, not in the paucity, but in the vastness of the materials, and in the labour of collecting and classifying them.

Although the Key itself could be used by none but students acquainted with Greek and Hebrew, the use of the Key can be made apparent to readers knowing nothing but English—and this by a single example, with only a few words of preface.

[4] Hebrew manuscripts in the first century were written without vowels. In the sixth or seventh century substitutes for vowels (called vowel-points) began to be introduced,[1] but when the first Hebrew Gospel was written, these substitutes did not exist. Under these circumstances, ambiguity and error could hardly be avoided even if the consonants were clearly distinguishable, as we may

---

[1] Dr. Ginsburg's *Introduction to the Hebrew Bible*, p. 451.

easily realise if we try to imagine the consequences if in English we were left to infer from the context the meaning of *bt, frm, wnt*, or *mst*.[1]

[5] But, further, many of the Hebrew consonants are hardly distinguishable, e.g. *h* and *ch* (ה and ח), and *d* and *r* (ד and ר). We ought not to be surprised at the multitude of errors arising from the latter of these similarities. Not only do we find the Hebrew Ramah, Madon, etc., represented by the Greek Daman, Marron, etc., but in parallel Hebrew books, and even in different passages of the same Hebrew book, the same person is called Hadadezer and Hadarezer.[2]

---

[1] [4a] For the consideration of the instances of confusion of Hebrew letters to be hereafter given, the following extracts from Dr. Ginsburg's *Introduction to the Hebrew Bible* may be found useful by readers acquainted with Hebrew:—

(i.) *Concerning quiescent letters.*—"It is now established beyond a doubt that the letters אהוי, commonly called quiescent or feeble letters, have been gradually introduced into the Hebrew text. It is, moreover, perfectly certain that the presence or absence of these letters in our text in many instances is entirely due to the idiosyncrasy of the Scribes" (p. 136).

(ii.) *Concerning y.*—"Very frequently it was not expressed in the primitive forms. This orthography is still exhibited in the name בל *Bel*=בעל *Baal* which has survived in three instances (Is. xlvi. 1, Jer. l. 2, li. 44) apart from compound proper names, and in the particle of entreaty בי=בעי *I pray, O!*" (p. 142).

(iii.) *Concerning* א *and y.*—"That the א and y, like the ב and כ, the ו and י, etc., must have been similar in form in olden times is evident from" a "caution" which Dr. Ginsburg quotes as "given in the Talmud to the Scribes," and he adds instances of their interchangeableness (pp. 143-4).

(iv.) *Concerning words written "plene," i.e. with quiescent letters, or "defective" (i.e. without them).*—"When the scribe was in doubt whether a word is to be written plene or defective, he naturally wrote it plene, since he thereby committed no mistake even if the word in question ought properly to have been written defective" (p. 157).

[4b] Some of these confusions may have arisen from the Samaritan characters of the old version of the Bible. But as late as the first century (*Hor. Heb.* vol. i. p. 170), Galilaeans confused (1) א, y, and ח, (2) ב and כ. The Jerusalem Talmud says, "The mystical doctors distinguished not between *Cheth* and *He*," and the Babylonian says, "The schools of Eleazar ben Jacob pronounced *Aleph Ain*, and *Ain Aleph*."

[2] 2 S. viii. 3-12 (Hebr.) "Hadadezer"; (LXX) "Hadraazar"; but 2 S. x. 16, 19, etc., and elsewhere in Scripture and Josephus, "Hadarezer."

[6] It happens that this last variation causes no serious historical difficulty. But now take the similarity between the Hebrew name for Syria, *i.e.* Aram, and the Hebrew for Idumæa, *i.e.* Edom.[1] The former and the latter are represented severally by *a'rm* (ארם) and *a'dm* (אדם). No knowledge of Hebrew, nothing but common sense, is needed to convince us that, unless the context made the meaning absolutely certain, errors would arise from this similarity. Hence we cannot be surprised that where the second book of Samuel speaks of "*Syria* and Moab," Chronicles has "*Edom* and Moab," and the Septuagint "Idumæa" in both cases.[2] In another passage, where the Revised Version gives "Syrians" in the text and "Edomites" in the margin, the Septuagint prefers the latter, and in another, where the Hebrew has certainly "Syria," the Greek gives "Edom."[3] Again, the title of the sixtieth Psalm represents David as striving with "Aram," *i.e.* with the Syrians, and then adds that Joab returned and "smote of *Edom* . . . twelve thousand." Here the Septuagint, while translating what refers to Syria, omits what refers to Edom, perhaps taking it as an erroneous repetition of the statement about Syria. It follows from these facts that if, in two parallel Greek documents bearing on Jewish history, we find Idumæa in one and Syria in another, this must be taken as evidence pointing to translation from Hebrew. One such instance would, of course, not suffice to prove translation. But it ought to prepare us to study the text with a view to ascertain whether other deviations may be similarly explained.

---

[1] For the convenience of readers ignorant of Hebrew, א will sometimes be transliterated as *a'*, and ע as *a''*. It must be remembered that Hebrew words are read from right to left.

[2] 2 S. viii. 11-12 (also 13), 1 Chr. xviii. 11.

[3] 2 K. xvi. 6, 1 K. xi. 25.

§ 3. *Specimens of Greek error arising from confusion of similar Hebrew letters*

Without some knowledge of Hebrew and Greek it would be impossible to use to any good purpose the Key above described. But a few specimens of its results may be helpful. For besides indicating the astonishing extent to which the Septuagint is permeated with error, they will also show how natural the mistakes were, and how probable it is that other translators might err in the same way.

[7] Here are some instances arising from confusions of the following six Hebrew roots: (i.) " feed," " pasture," " shepherd " ; (ii.) " know," cause to know," " teach," " knowledge," " wise," etc. ; (iii.) " evil " ; (iv.) " appoint a meeting with," " meet," " appointment " ; (v.) " break " ; (vi.) " cry out." A glance at the footnote will convince readers, with or without knowledge of Hebrew, that such confusions are very natural.[1]

Is. xliv. 20: " He *feedeth on* ashes." LXX "*Know* thou that ashes. . . ."

Prov. xv. 14: "The mouth of fools *feedeth on* folly." LXX "The mouth of the unlearned *will know* evil things."

Prov. x. 21: " The lips of the righteous *feed* many." LXX " The lips of the righteous *understand* lofty things."

Is. xliv. 28: "He that saith of Cyrus, [He is] my *shepherd*." LXX " He that saith to Cyrus *to be wise*."

Jer. iii. 15 : " They shall feed you with *knowledge* and understanding." LXX "They shall shepherd you, *shepherding* with understanding."

Jer. vi. 18: " Hear, ye nations, and *know*, O congregation, what is among them." LXX " The nations heard and *those shepherding* their flocks."

Hos. xiii. 5: "I did *know* thee in the wilderness." LXX " I did *shepherd* thee in the wilderness."

Ezek. xix. 7: " And he *knew*." LXX " And he *fed on*."[2]

---

[1] The Hebrew is (i.) רעה, (ii.) ידע, (iii.) רע, (iv.) יעד, (v.) רעע, (vi.) רוע.

[2] Ezek. xix. 7, καὶ ἐνέμετο τῷ θράσει αὐτοῦ.

Prov. xiii. 19: "To depart from *evil*." LXX "Far from *knowledge*."
Prov. xix. 23: "He shall not be visited with *evil*." LXX "Where *knowledge* does not visit."
2 S. xix. 7 (Hebr. 8): "And that will be *worse* (lit. *evil*) unto thee than all." LXX "And *know* for thyself, and evil for thee this, more than all."[1]
Prov. xix. 27: "Words of *knowledge*." LXX "*Evil* speeches."
Is. xxviii. 9: "Whom will he teach *knowledge*." LXX "To whom did we announce *evil* things?"
Eccles. vii. 22: "For oftentimes also thine own heart *knoweth*." LXX "For very often it will do thee *evil*, and on many occasions will thy heart do *mischief*."[2]
Dan. xii. 4: "*Knowledge*." LXX (but not (32) Theod.) "*Unrighteousness*."
Mic. iv. 9: "Wherefore dost thou *cry out aloud* (lit. *a cry*)?" LXX "Wherefore didst thou *know evil things*?"
Ex. xxix. 42-43: "I will *meet* (lit. *appoint*) with you ... I will meet with the children of Israel." LXX "I will *be known* to thee ... I will appoint to the children of Israel." [Here the LXX, as is often the case with scribes, makes a mistake at first, which, when the circumstances recur soon afterwards, it does not repeat.]
Ex. xxx. 36 (and comp. Num. xvii. 4): "I will *meet* with you." LXX "I will be *known* to thee."
Am. iii. 3: "Except they have *agreed* (marg. made an *appointment*)." LXX "Except they have made themselves *known*."
Hos. xii. 1 (Hebr. 2): "Ephraim *feedeth on* wind." LXX "Ephraim [is] an *evil* spirit."
Is. lvi. 11: "And these are *shepherds*." LXX "And they are *evil*."
Jer. xv. 12: "Can one *break* iron?" LXX "Shall iron be *known*?"
Jer. ii. 16: "They have *broken* (marg. *fed on*)." LXX "They *knew* thee."
Prov. xi. 15: "(He) shall be *sore broken*," lit. "*breaking* shall be broken." LXX "A *wicked* man *doeth evil*."

[1] The LXX has combined (20) the wrong meaning ("know") with the right one ("evil").
[2] The LXX has again (20) combined two meanings.

Prov. xxv. 19: "A *broken* tooth." LXX "The way of the *wicked*."

[8] Errors arising from neglect of Hebrew grammatical distinctions—*e.g.* that between causative and non-causative forms of the verb—do not, strictly speaking, come within the scope of this section. But as the word "know" has been under consideration, and as it may be necessary hereafter to consider possible confusions in the New Testament between "know" and "cause to know," *i.e.* "say," "teach," etc., it will be well to add one or two instances of such confusion here:—

Is. xix. 12: "And let them *know*." LXX "And let them *say*."
Is. xlviii. 6: "And thou didst not *know* them." LXX "And thou didst not *say*."
Ex. vi. 3: "But [by] my name I was not *known*." LXX "But my name I did not *show*."

§ 4. *Specimens of Greek error arising from confusion of similar Hebrew words*

It would be possible to repeat the process of the last section with regard to other letters and other groups of words. But want of space prevents us from mentioning more than a few that are most frequently confused.

[9] (i.) The word (*a*) "sit" is identical, in some of its forms, with (*b*) "turn," "return," "do again," and hence "again." In Num. xi. 4, Deut. i. 45, Josh. v. 2, Judg. xix. 7, 2 S. xix. 37, Job vi. 29, Zech. ix. 12, the Revised Version has "turn," "return," "again," "the second time"; but the LXX has in every case "sit." Also the word "sit" is regularly used for "abide," "remain," "sojourn."[1]

This may be important, in view of passages where

---

[1] "Sit (ישב)," "Return (שוב)": but "he will return" (ישב or ישוב) may be identical with "sit." "Sitting" is שבת, which may be confused with "rest" and "sabbath."

Jesus is described as "sitting," or "returning," or doing a thing "again," by one, but not all of the Synoptists; or where the Synoptists describe Peter as "sitting" during his denial of our Lord, while John describes him as "standing." An interesting instance of variation *in Hebrew*, bearing on these forms, may be found in two parallel Hebrew passages,[1] one saying "Jeroboam *dwelt in* Egypt," but the other "Jeroboam *returned from* Egypt."

[10] (ii.) The words "friend," or "companion," and "evil," are identical and repeatedly confused. This will come before us in connection with passages where Matthew represents a king, or lord, as calling a wicked servant "companion."[2]

[11] (iii.) The words "there," "name," "put," "wonder," "hear," "report," "fame," "announce [the Gospel]" are very similar, and are often confused. This has a bearing on passages where one evangelist mentions "*wondering*," or "*dismay*," and another "*hearing*"; and where one says that Jesus "came *announcing* [the Gospel]," and another that "the *report* of Jesus came" into a certain district.[3]

[12] (iv.) The words "cross," "across," "ford," "ferryboat," "evening," "Arabah" (often called "wilderness," or "lowland," or "plain") are very liable to confusion, and some of them are frequently confused not only by the Septuagint but in the Hebrew. Thus, where the Hebrew text gives "Lodge not *at the fords*," the Hebrew margin gives "*in the plains*"; and the Septuagint, adopting the latter, treats it as a proper name "Araboth."[4] This may have a bearing on several synoptic passages where one

---

[1] [9a] 1 K. xii. 2, 2 Ch. x. 2, וישב in both cases. "From (-מ)" and "in (-ב)" are frequently (158 a) confused. In Kings, Codex Alexandrinus mistranslates, or conforms to Chronicles. [2] The Hebrew is רע (see 188).

[3] "There" = שם, "name" = שם, "put" = שים, "hear" = שמע, "wonder" = שמם.

[4] 2 S. xvii. 16. In 2 S. xix. 18 (Heb. 19), "there went over *a ferry boat* (marg. *convoy*)," the LXX (confusing *d* with *r*) renders the word by *two* meanings (*a*) "service," (*b*) "crossing," and combines them.

evangelist, unsupported by the rest, mentions a "boat," or describes Jesus as "passing along."

§ 5. *The place of Christ's baptism: Bethabara? Betharaba? or Bethany?*

[13] In view of the perplexed question as to the place of Christ's baptism, importance attaches to the following mentions of the Jordan: "*the plains of* (Heb. *Araboth*) Moab which are *by* the Jordan at Jericho," "*the plains of* (Heb. *Araboth*) Moab *beyond* the Jordan at Jericho eastward,"[1] while the Septuagint in both cases appears to treat "*Araboth* of Moab" as a place, and certainly does so in the former passage, "*Araboth* of Moab which is by Jordan at Jericho." Mark apparently mentions the baptism as occurring in Jordan,[2] and Matthew describes Jesus as coming towards Jordan to be baptized; but Luke omits all mention of the Jordan in this connection, having however previously said, "John came into all the *surrounding country* of the Jordan." John defines "the place where John was baptizing" as "*Bethany* beyond Jordan." But there are various readings "Bethabara," and "Betharaba." Bethany may mean "the place of a ship," Bethabara "the place of a ford or ferryboat," Betharaba "a place in the Arabah." The latter name is given in Joshua several times to a city in the "wilderness" of Judah; but the Hebrew itself once erroneously drops "Beth," and calls it simply "the Arabah," *i.e.* "the wilderness," and the Greek, on another occasion, substitutes "Bethabara" (as some suppose, correctly).[3]

[14] Origen, visiting the Jordan early in the third

[1] Num. xxxi. 12, Josh. xiii. 32.
[2] Mk. i. 9 ἐβαπτίσθη εἰς τὸν' I., lit. "he was baptized (in)to Jordan," may mean "he came to Jordan and was baptized," or "was baptized by Jordan," *i.e.*, on the banks of, or near, the river. Mk. i. 5 has ἐβαπτίζοντο ἐν τῷ Ἰορδάνῃ.
[3] *Ency. Bib.*, "Beth-Arabah." In Josh. xv. 61, LXX (but not A) has "Tharabaam."

century, found no trace of any "Bethany" in the neighbourhood of Jordan, but adds, "They say that *Bethabara* is indicated, on the banks of the Jordan, and that John is said to have baptized there." This testimony is not lightly to be disputed. Yet Origen himself tells us that "Bethany" was supported by "almost all the copies," and by Heracleon. It is not intended here to discuss which reading is historically correct, but merely to indicate that the variations point to a confusion arising from a Hebrew original.[1]

§ 6. *On the evidence required to prove translation from Hebrew in the Synoptic Gospels*

The reader may be disposed to infer from the preceding instances of Septuagint mistranslation that it must be a very short and simple process to detect translation in the Gospels if it is actually latent there: "only give us three or four such instances as those of Edom above and we will be convinced at once."

[15] This is a very natural way of looking at the matter, but it ignores some important differences between the Greek of the New Testament and that particular Greek version of the Old Testament which is commonly called the Septuagint —differences that would explain why errors would be more speedily corrected, and obliterated for posterity, in the former than in the latter.

In the first place, large parts of the Greek Old Testament, partly because of their inferior interest and partly because of their extent, would be comparatively rarely read by Greek-speaking Jews or Christians; and consequently less notice would be attracted by the mistakes in them.

[1] It is possible that "Bethabara" may be historically, and "Bethany" textually, correct. If the two terms may mean the same thing, John may have taken advantage of a transitory local appellation, or even of a literary paraphrase, in order to call attention to a kind of mystical appropriateness in the name: Christ began His course at one Bethany and brought it toward its end at another.

SPECIMENS OF ERROR

In the second place, the Old Testament does not contain parallel versions of the words of Isaiah, Jeremiah, etc., corresponding to the parallel versions of the words of Christ in our Gospels.[1] In the latter, parallelism, together with occasional diversity, would lead a Christian editor to correct the diversity if it arose from mistranslation. In the former there would be no such cause for correction.

In the third place, the Septuagint had existed for more than three centuries before controversies began between Jews and Christians about the meaning of Hebrew Scriptures. Up to the middle of the first century (A.D.) there was no controversial inducement to correct Greek errors. The Alexandrian Jew, Philo, regarded the Septuagint as inspired. Probably many Greek-speaking Jews agreed with him, and certainly the Palestinian Jews took no steps to correct the Greek errors. Not till the Alexandrian Apollos began to "mightily convince" Greek-speaking Jews that Jesus was the Messiah, by quoting from the Scriptures, and not till Christian evangelists throughout Asia Minor freely appealed to the Septuagint, and finally published Gospels quoting from it, would the Hebrew-reading Jews, who adhered to the Jewish faith, be roused to protest.

But protests were not followed by action till early in the second century, when there appeared "a new translation, slavishly literal in character, made by a Jewish proselyte of the name of Aquila."[2] But it was too late.

[1] In the parallel books of *Kings* and *Chronicles*, diversities have been occasionally corrected by the Greek translators. But the inducement to make such corrections was comparatively slight in such cases—often mere statistics, or names. See 16.

[2] Robertson Smith's *The Old Testament in the Jewish Church*, p. 76. Aquila's translation is described on p. 391 as "made expressly in the interests of Jewish exegesis." "Symmachus," the author continues, "and Theodotion followed later, but still in the second century. . . . Aquila, says Jerome, sought to reproduce the Hebrew word for word; Symmachus aimed at a clear expression of the sense; while Theodotion rather sought to give a revised edition not very divergent from the Greek of the Septuagint."

The Christian Church was by this time committed to the Septuagint. In the middle of the second century we find Justin Martyr bitterly attacking the Jews for "corrupting" the Hebrew Scriptures, simply because the Jews adhered to the Hebrew and rejected the erroneous Greek![1] It was not till the third century that an attempt was made by a Christian writer, Origen, to show the divergences of the Septuagint from the Hebrew; and his work was not so far appreciated by the Christians as to induce them to preserve it for posterity.

[16] How different was the case with the New Testament! Reading daily, and catechizing in, and preaching from, and disputing about, and knowing by heart, their brief and recently composed Gospels, many early Christian evangelists may well have desired to compare and blend them into a harmonious whole as Tatian did some time after the middle of the second century. Others—who did not venture to intermix the Gospel texts in the form of a continuous harmony—would write on the margin of one Gospel the parallel expression used by another. These marginal notes might be taken as additions or corrections by some scribe copying the manuscript a few years afterwards. In that case, they would either be added to the text, or else they would supplant the text.[2] The general result would be to obliterate for posterity most of the striking instances of discrepancy arising from obvious mistranslation.

Again, the text of the Greek New Testament—instead of being allowed to retain its errors of mistranslation (if errors there are) until three centuries had made them venerable and secured their perpetuation—was plunged almost from the beginning into a furnace of controversy. A few specimens of attacks made upon the Christian Gospels

[1] *Tryph.* 72-3.
[2] [16a] From the latter cause arises the curious result that sometimes a manuscript (as, for example, the Codex Bezae) shows a text of Mark conformed to that of Luke, while the parallel Luke is conformed to Mark!

are still extant—preserved only in the works of those Christian Apologists who quote in order to refute them. But we have to bear in mind that controversy must have been at work from the time when Christianity began to attract the notice of educated Greeks and Romans: and its effect on evangelists must have been in the direction of harmonizing and correction of error—except in cases where the error was too old to be corrected.

No doubt, in the Hebrew books of Kings and Chronicles flagrant discrepancies have been allowed by the Septuagint as well as by the Jewish editors to remain uncorrected. But in the first place, there was little inducement to correct these. No great questions of religion depended on them. They were mostly matters for Jews alone, and the Jewish mind was less alive than the Greek to errors of statistics, and names, and prosaic facts. No controversies raged about the dimensions of the Temple or the chronology of the kings of Israel and Judah. In the next place, it should be noted that in several instances the Greek translators of Kings and Chronicles *have* corrected discrepancies created by the Jewish writers. Much more was this to be expected in Greek evangelists translating, or editing translations, from a variously interpreted Hebrew original.

[17] To these three differences—(i.) familiarity arising from brevity and from frequent repetition, (ii.) the existence of parallel Gospels, at first perhaps adopted severally in several Churches and only gradually adopted by all, and harmonized by some, (iii.) the influence of controversy tending to the removal of errors and discrepancies—must be added two others: (iv.) that of oral tradition, at first, and in a few Churches, Aramaic, but afterwards, and in many more, Greek, (v.) the absence, at first, of one written and supremely authoritative Gospel.

Summing up, we may say that the earliest Greek translations of the *Logia* would be for some time fluid, like the versions of Daniel, which, as given by the Septuagint and by Theodotion, are, in some parts, practically different books. At first, causes (iv.) and (v.) would tend to differentiation, covering up the Hebrew original with variations and amplifications. Then, causes (i.), (ii.), and (iii.) would tend to assimilation, sometimes returning to the original Hebrew, sometimes departing from it, but in either case cancelling those discrepancies which before made a Hebrew origin obvious. For example, two early parallel Gospels may have had " Idumaea " and " Syria " respectively. Later editors may have removed the discrepancy by substituting " Idumaea " for " Syria," and in so doing they may have rightly returned to the original Hebrew. But what is the consequence ? The proofs of mistranslation from an original Hebrew text will now have vanished.

[18] Nevertheless a great deal of evidence attesting translation from Hebrew still remains, not difficult to perceive when we are prepared for it, and, when perceived, conclusive. Only we must not expect to find the Gospels agreeing together quite as closely as Ezra and the first book of Esdras, or as the Septuagint version of Daniel with Theodotion. When the same or nearly the same words occur in parallel passages, we must be prepared to find the context or construction different, as at the outset of the Gospel, where Mark says, "*there went out to him* [the Baptist] all the Judaean country," Matthew "*there went out to him* . . . all Judaea and all the surrounding country of the Jordan," Luke "*he* [the Baptist] *came to* all the surrounding country of the Jordan "—differences that could easily be explained by the obscurities of Hebrew syntax and paralleled from the Septuagint.[1]

[19] When translated from Hebrew, speech may easily become narrative, and narrative speech ; future things past, and past future ; subject may become object, and object

---

[1] Mk. i. 5, Mt. iii. 5, Lk. iii. 3 (335*b*).

subject; "for" may be replaced by "though," "and" by "but," the interrogative by the affirmative, passive by active, active by passive, and either of these by the causative. It would take up far too much space to give instances here of each of these deviations: they will better be reserved for special passages of the Gospels, to be discussed later, on which they severally have a bearing. But there is one source of confusion so important that it must be examined immediately, because it permeates the Septuagint and may reasonably be supposed to affect the earliest Gospels still more extensively. This will be considered in the next chapter.

CHAPTER II

THE ERROR OF CONFLATION

§ 1. *Conflations, their nature and origin*

[20] A "CONFLATION" (literally "something blown or fused together"), when used as a literary technical term, ought etymologically to mean a fusion of two renderings in one. As a fact, the name is frequently given to such a combination of two or more meanings as does not amount to fusion. For example, in a passage in the book of the Son of Sirach, commonly called Ecclesiasticus, where the Hebrew has "drought," the Greek has "mountains and deserts." Now the Hebrew "drought" means also "a dry or desolate place," and might be translated "deserts." But how are we to explain the addition "mountains and"? The answer is given by the remark of the editors, who tell us that *the Hebrew scribe has written* "(*of the*) *mountains*" *above the line*. The Hebrew of "mountain" is very like the first two letters of "drought," and the scribe seems to have suggested this as an alternative. The Greek text combines the two in what is called a *conflation*.[1]

---

[1] [20*a*] Sir. xliii. 21, "drought" (חרב), "mountains"=הרים. The antiquity of the lately discovered Hebrew of Ecclesiasticus appears to be demonstrated by recent discussions, and is assumed throughout this work. "Sir." is an abbreviation of "Sirachides," *i.e.* son of Sirach, and is preferred to "Ecclesiasticus," because the latter, when abridged, is liable to be confused with abridgments of "Ecclesiastes." The Hebrew of xxxix. 15 to xlix. 11 is edited by Cowley and Neubauer, Oxford, 1897; some earlier and later chapters, by Schechter and Taylor, Cambridge, 1899.

THE ERROR OF CONFLATION

[21] Another Hebrew passage in the same book says, "with all your heart sing aloud," but the Greek says, "we sang with all our heart *and voice*"; in a third, where the Hebrew has "count," the Greek has "in number *and measure.*" The Hebrew of "voice" is quite different from that of "heart," and so is the Hebrew of "number" from the Hebrew of "measure." But *both these additions are found in the Hebrew margin.* In the former, the scribe was influenced by literalism, feeling that people do not sing with their "heart" but with their "voice"; in the latter, he perhaps desired to complete the meaning.[1]

[22] These instances give us some notion of the processes that result in conflation. The owner of the manuscript jots down in the margin some various reading if the text is doubtful, or some explanatory term or amplification if the text is obscure or incomplete, never dreaming, perhaps, of the danger of its being hereafter added to the text. Then a scribe or translator, ignorant of the writer's motive, and regarding the marginal note either as a part of the text accidentally omitted, or else as an authoritative addition, transfers it to the text.

[23] The earliest Christian ecclesiastical writer, Papias, is perhaps apologising for Mark's redundancy when he says that the Evangelist "committed no fault . . . for he made it his one object *neither to omit anything of what he had heard nor to misstate anything therein.*"[2] The italicised words at all events express that sense of responsibility which, when accompanied by a want of exact and first-hand knowledge, naturally leads a scrupulous translator or scribe into the error of conflation. "The text may be right," he

---

[1] Sir. xxxix. 35, xlii. 7.
[2] Euseb. *H.E.* iii. 39, 15 (quoting Papias), ὥστε οὐδὲν ἥμαρτε Μάρκος οὕτως ἔνια γράψας ὡς ἀπεμνημόνευσεν. ἑνὸς γὰρ ἐποιήσατο πρόνοιαν, τοῦ μηδὲν ὧν ἤκουσε παραλιπεῖν ἢ ψεύσασθαί τι ἐν αὐτοῖς. For the meaning of this, see *Ency. Bib.*, "Gospels," § 65.

says, "but so may the margin be. It will be best to put down both."

§ 2. *Conflations, mostly caused by obscurity*

Of the three instances given above from Ecclesiasticus only one was caused by possible doubt as to the Hebrew text. The two others were of an explanatory or amplificatory nature.

[24] But this does not represent the facts in most of the *canonical* books of the Septuagint.[1] Presumably the Hebrew text of those was regarded as more authoritative than the Hebrew of the son of Sirach. At all events in the canonical books the Septuagint seems seldom to depart deliberately from the Hebrew, except to correct expressions that may have appeared erroneous or unseemly, *e.g.* anthropomorphisms applied to God, as when it alters "it grieved him [*i.e.* God] *at his heart*," into "he considered [it]."[2] In these rare instances there was seldom any temptation to conflate. The translators or editors might naturally feel that they had expressed the substantial meaning of the Hebrew by a reverent paraphrase. Why should they spoil their work by adding a literal rendering that would shock Greek readers? But where an obscure Hebrew passage had been either loosely paraphrased or erroneously translated, there an editor of the translation might naturally step in to add a marginal correction, and a scribe might subsequently incorporate it in the text.

[25] In exceptional cases conflation, sometimes on a large scale, is caused by supplementary tradition, as in the story of Jeroboam, where the Septuagint gives two considerably divergent accounts of the way in which he became king. Many more such cases may be expected in the Synoptic Gospels. Just as, in the case of Jeroboam, one

[1] Daniel is an exception. That is freely amplified and interpolated by the LXX; Job less freely. [2] Gen. vi. 6, διενοήθη, comp. viii. 21.

tradition might prevail in Judah and another in Israel, so, as regards some of the words and acts of Jesus, the Galilaean Church might in the earliest times preserve one account and the Church in Jerusalem another. But it is shown by experience that, even where supplementary tradition intervenes, many diverging expressions in two parallel narratives of the Septuagint may be explained by mistranslation from Hebrew. The following instance is of great interest because it presents in the Septuagint a Greek story of which the Hebrew original has been lost—a story manifestly corrupt and inconsistent, but believed by many scholars to represent the earliest tradition more faithfully than the Hebrew version that has been preserved:—

1 Kings xi. 29 foll. (Heb.)

[26] The story of Ahijah (before Jeroboam's flight to Egypt).

"And he [Jeroboam or Ahijah [2]] had clad himself in a new garment . . . And Ahijah caught the new garment that was on him[self] and rent it [in] twelve pieces and he said to Jeroboam, Take thee ten pieces . . ." [Then comes a long discourse with frequent mention of David.]

1 Kings (LXX only) xii. 24 (o) [1]

The story of Samaia (after Jeroboam's return from Egypt).

"The word of the Lord came to Samaia the [? son of] Enlamei, saying, *Take to thyself* (a_1) a *new* garment, (a_2) *that which has not passed into water*,[3] and *rend it* [in] twelve pieces, and *thou shalt give* it to Jeroboam and shalt say to him, Thus saith the Lord, Take to thyself *twelve* pieces to clothe thee. And

---

[1] For this passage, see Swete's edition of the LXX, vol. i. pp. 708-710. The verses are xii. 24 (*a*)-xii. 24 (*z*).

[2] The last person mentioned is Ahijah, so that "he" would most naturally mean the prophet. It is so understood by LXX, which inserts "Ahijah."

[3] ἱμάτιον καινὸν τὸ οὐκ εἰσεληλυθὸς εἰς ὕδωρ. The letters a_1, a_2, denote (probably) two translations of one early Hebrew original.

Jeroboam took [them]. And Samaia said, Thus saith the Lord concerning the ten tribes of Israel." [Hereupon follows a version of the people's remonstrance to Rehoboam, "And the people said . . ."]

[27] Here the version preserved by the Septuagint alone, contains many traces of superior antiquity. It retains the homely expression about a garment that has never yet "gone to the wash" as we say in English, though it adds the free rendering "new."[1] It also retains the manifestly erroneous "twelve" instead of "ten," caused by mechanical repetition of the preceding "twelve" or by corruption of the Greek.[2]

[28] As regards the change of the imperative, "Take a new garment," to the statement of fact, "and he had clad" and "caught," we may compare a passage that comes a little later where a prophet is speaking, and the Septuagint has, "And he shall sacrifice on thee . . . and he shall burn men's bones on thee, and *he shall give* a sign"; but in reality the speech of the prophet terminates at "thee," and the following words should run "and *he gave* a sign." Hence it is easy to understand that an original "Take" may have been interpreted (a_1) "and he took" [*i.e.* "clad himself with"], (a_2) "and he caught," and this the author of the extant Hebrew version appears to have done (**240**), and to have conflated the two meanings.

[29] The Septuagint version omits the long moralising discourse about the mercies of God to the house of David.

---

[1] Comp. Mk. ii. 21 (Mt. ix. 16), ἀγνάφου "that has never gone to the fuller," where Lk. v. 36 has simply "new."

[2] [27*a*] "To thyself twelve," σεαυτῷ δώδεκα. Possibly the original -τω δεκα (ω being casually repeated) was written -τωωδεκα which suggested -τω δωδεκα. "Corruption of the Greek" will henceforth be called, for brevity, "Greek corruption."

But this may be because the tradition preserved in the Septuagint originated from Ephraim, that in the Hebrew from Judah.

§ 3. *Rules for returning through a conflation to the Original*

[30] The consideration of the stories of Ahijah and Samaia leads us to one excellent rule in attempting to decide between the claims of two clauses in a conflation, viz., "Choose the more difficult, or the less commonplace." The tendency of later versions is to remove whatever is rough, homely, or unseemly, and to substitute the easy and edifying. Thus, above, in the story of Samaia, if "new" and "never yet gone to the water" constitute a conflation, the latter is more likely to represent the original Hebrew. So, too, in Mark,[1] the phrase, "that has not been fulled," is probably older than the corresponding "new" in Luke. On this point one of the best instances is from Latin, quoted in Bacon's *Advancement of Learning* concerning a scribe who altered the phrase in the Epistle to the Corinthians, "let down by *a basket* (sportam)" into "let down by *the gate* (portam)." "Sporta" was comparatively unknown, "porta" well known, and it is a universal tendency in scribes to substitute the well known for the less known.

[31] Another general rule will appear to be deducible from the instances to be hereafter given : *the correct rendering in a conflation mostly follows the incorrect one.* For this, a very natural reason may be given. In the majority of cases of conflation, the text has been wrong and a marginal reading has set it right.[2] But when a scribe was copying a

---

[1] Mk. ii. 21 quoted above in footnote.

[2] In a few cases, a scribe or editor may be peculiarly eccentric and fond of novelty, introducing erroneous corrections in the margin. But that would be comparatively rare in the Septuagint, where the Hebrew was of very high authority, and the written text was not liable to be largely supplemented by oral traditions. The tendency of the corrector there would generally be to return to the literal Hebrew where the Greek had deviated from it.

manuscript and mistook a marginal correction for an addition, it was very natural that, in transferring it to the text, he should place it second, not first. The old clause would seem to have a sort of claim to precedence, and, apart from sentiment, the new clause, being of the nature of an appendix or supplement, would naturally come last.[1]

§ 4. *Conflation mostly the sign of an early translation*

[32] The Septuagint translation, which is generally said to have been made in the third century before Christ,[2] is far less accurate than such parts as have come down to us from the versions of Aquila and Theodotion, composed in the second century after Christ. In particular, the Septuagint version of Daniel abounds with conflations that are excluded by Theodotion. In the Septuagint itself, some books are far more faithful to the original than others: for example, the Septuagint version of Ezra is superior, both in general accuracy and in freedom from conflations, to the parallel work in the Septuagint, called the First Book of Esdras. The dates of these two translations are not known from external evidence. But internal evidence suggests that the translation of Ezra is the later.

[33] The oldest manuscript of the Septuagint, the Codex Vaticanus, is often (though not always) less close to the Hebrew than the later Codex Alexandrinus; and the latter rejects many of the conflations incorporated in the former.

[34] On the other hand, a version of the Septuagint was

---

[1] [31a] This applies merely to *marginal* additions. *Interlinear* additions might be regarded as part of the original text and would be inserted in the text according to their position in its columns. In the Ecclesiasticus conflations above-quoted (20), the two Hebrew *marginal* additions came last, but the *interlinear* first, in their several Greek conflations.

[2] It is not probable, however, that all the books of the Bible were translated into Greek at the same time.

published in the third century, after Origen's death, by Lucianus of Antioch. He is said to have espoused the cause of the literal, as distinct from the allegorical, interpretation of Scripture ; and perhaps he entered on his task with a bias against Origen's scholastic labours. At all events Lucianus' work teems with conflations and precludes us from laying it down as an invariable rule that a conflative version is earlier than a non-conflative one.

[35] But, as a whole, applying to the Gospels the analogy of the Septuagint, we should say that, if the former were translated from, or corrected by, a Hebrew original, the Hebrew would be at first freely and inaccurately translated into Greek ; and the earlier translations, among other features of inaccuracy, would contain more numerous conflations than the later.

CHAPTER III

CONFLATIONS OF NAMES

*§ 1. *Specimens of name-conflation*[1]

[36] The Septuagint's name-conflations, and its general confusion of names, may be of great historical importance if they can explain why the later Gospels omit many of the names in Mark, *e.g.* Bartimaeus, Boanerges, Abiathar, Dalmanoutha, and Levi. Moreover, name-conflations show with special clearness what Hebrew letters are most liable to be confused. When a word *with a meaning* is confused with another, the scribe may be biassed by the meaning; but when a word *with no meaning* is confused with another, there is seldom any cause for the confusion except similarity of letters.

Here are a few specimens of name-confusion resulting in name-conflation :—

[37] 2 S. xxiv. 6 : "Dan-jaan"; LXX, "Dan-eidan and Oudan." [Codex *A* "Jaran and Ioudan."]

Ezra viii. 10 : "*Sons of* Shelomith"; LXX gives this correctly, but Codex *A* conflates "sons-of (Heb. *Baani*)," taking it first as "sons of," and then as part of the father's name, "(a_1) *sons of* (a_2) *Baani*-seleimmouth."

The parallel 1 Esdr. viii. 36 has "*sons of Banias,* Saleimoth*"* (A, "*sons of Bani,* Assalimoth ").

---

[1] For the meaning of the asterisk, see p. xix. n. But **36** and **45** will be found useful to the general reader. The letters a_1 and a_2 denote two Greek renderings of one Hebrew original.

Dan. viii. 16: "Gabri-el," lit. "man of God," is rightly given as "Gabriel" by Theodotion. But the LXX has (a_1) "Gabriel," and (a_2) " man to "—because the same Hebrew word means either " God " or " to."[1]

[38] Ezra iv. 8-9: " Rehum *the chancellor*," lit. " master of judgment " (Heb. *Ba"l-Ta"m*). This is translated in the first book of Esdras (1 Esdr. ii. 15) " Rathumus and Beeltethmus," (*ib*. ii. 21) " Rathumus (a_1) who writes the things that come before him, and (a_2) Beeltethmus," (*ib*. ii. 16) " Rathumus who (sic) the things that come before him." (In Ezra it is translated "Raoul Badatamen" and "Raoum Baal.")

Josh. vii. 24: " Unto the *valley* (Heb. *Emek*) of Achor"; LXX, " Unto the (a_1) *ravine* of Achor . . . unto (a_2) *Emek-achor*."

Ezra vii. 13 (Aramaic): " And (the) *Levites* " is correctly rendered. But the parallel 1 Esdr. viii. 10 has " (a_1) and the Levites (a_2) *and these*," the two words being somewhat similar.[2]

2 S. xv. 22: "' . . . and pass over.' And Ittai . . . passed over"; LXX, "' . . . and pass over (a_1) *with me*.' (a_2) And *Ittai* passed over. . . ." The same letters mean both " with me " and " Ittai."[3]

[39] 1 Chr. ii. 9-10: " . . . and Ram and Chelubai. And *Ram* begat *A*."; LXX, " and Ram and Chabel (a_1) *and Aram*. (a_2) *And Arran* begat *A*."

Judg. vi. 11: " The *Ab*iezrite." " Ab " (or " Abi ") means

---

[1] This induces LXX to rewrite the whole of the clause containing the name. The first clause (A₁) follows the Hebrew, but the second (A₂) reproduces the Hebrew word for word in a different sentence with a wrong meaning. The following is a literal translation: "(A₁) (a_1) And he called and said, (b_1) Gabri-el (c_1) instruct (d_1) that [man] [in] (e_1) the vision ; (A₂) (a_2) And having cried out said (b_2) *the man*, To (c_2) the ordinance (d_2) that (neut.) (e_2) the vision." The meaning of A₂ seems to be "The man said 'The vision is with a view to that ordinance'"; it follows the Hebrew literally, though wrongly (perhaps reading חקה " the ordinance " for הבן "instruct") and was perhaps thought by the conflator an improvement on the original. This is a case where the incorrect clause of a conflation comes second. [2] " And (the) Levites "= ללוא ; " and these "= ואלה. [3] " With me "=" Ittai "= אתי.

28

"father." Hence LXX, "The *father* of Esdrei." Codex *A* conflates "(a_1) The *father* of (a_2) A biezri." Judg. i. 15 : "*Caleb* gave her." " Ca-" may mean "according to," and "leb" may mean "heart." Hence LXX, "(a_1) *Caleb* gave to her (a_2) *according to her heart.*"

[40] In Judg. i. 27, "and her *towns*" is repeated six times. The R.V. marg. informs us that the literal translation is "and her *daughters*," the villages being regarded as "daughters" of the central town.

The LXX four times conflates "and her suburbs"[1] with "and her daughters" (in varying order), and twice has simply "and her daughters." Codex *A* has merely "and her daughters"—except in the first of the six instances, where it adds "and her scattered (hamlets)."

[41] Mic. vi. 16 : "the statutes of Omri"; LXX, "the laws of *my people* . . . the ordinances *of Zambrei*," the two words being similar.[2]

[42] 2 S. iii. 12 : "sent . . . *on his behalf*," marg. "*where he was*": an instance of the conversion of a phrase into (*a*) a name, as part of a triple conflate. The Hebrew means (a_1) "in the place of *a person*" (that is, "in his *behalf*") and (a_2) "in the place *where he was.*" But (a_2), in Greek, might suggest (a_3) "*immediately.*" The LXX first treats it as (*a*) a proper name, and then adds the meanings a_2 and a_3: "sent (*a*) to Thailam, (a_2) where he was, (a_3) immediately."[3]

[43] Judg. iv. 17 : "*Heber* the Kenite," LXX "(a_1) *Chaber*, (a_2) *a companion of* the Kenite" (or, "the Kenite companion "). The word "Chaber" means "companion." Codex *A* omits "companion."

---

[1] τὰ περίοικα αὐτῆς.   [2] My people (עמי)," " Omri (עמרי)."
[3] The Hebrew (txt.) is תחתו followed by לאמר ("saying"). Probably the LXX combined the ת, which begins the former, with the ל, which begins the latter. Instead of Θαιλαμ ου ην, "Thailam where he was," *A* has Θηλαμου γην, "the land of Thelamus"—an interesting instance of Greek corruption. The Greek αὐτόθεν "from the place," like our "on the spot," sometimes means "immediately."

[44] CONFLATIONS OF NAMES

[44] 1 S. xxi. 2 (Hebr. 3): "to such and such a place," LXX "in the place called (a_1) *God's Faith*, (a_2) Phellanei Maemoni." The Hebrew freely rendered "such and such" is "*Pelouni-Elmouni*," which has a very distant resemblance to a combination of "Elohim" (*i.e.* "God") and "Emunah" (*i.e.* "faith ").[1]

[45] One of the most remarkable instances of name-conflation is to be found in the list of David's eleven sons born in Jerusalem. The LXX *converts eleven to twenty-four*, adopting *two different versions*, represented below by i. and ii., and placing the whole of ii. after the whole of i., thus :—

2 S. v. 14-15

Hebr.	(1) Shammua,	(2) Shobab,	(3) Nathan,	(4) Solomon,	(5) Ibhar,
(i.) LXX	(1) Sammous,	(2) Sobab,	(3) Nathan,	(4) Salomon,	(5) Ebear,
(ii.) LXX	(1) Samae,	(2) Jesseibath,	(3) Nathan,	(4) Galamaan,	(5) Jebaar,
Hebr.	(6) Elishua,		(7) Nepheg,		(8) Japhia,
(i.) LXX	(6) El(e)isous,		(7) Naphek,		(8) Jephies,
(ii.) LXX	(6) (*a*) Theesous,	(*b*) Eliphalat,[2]	(7) (*a*) Naged,	(*b*) Naphek,	(8) Janatha,
Hebr.	(9) Elishama,	(10) Eliada,		(11) Eliphelet,	
(i.) LXX	(9) El(e)isama,	(10) Epidae,		(11) El(e)iphaath,	
(ii.) LXX	(9) Leasamus,	(10) Baaleimath,		(11) Eleiphaath,	

The second list is (33) omitted by Codex *A*. It is worth noting that the more inaccurate of the two Greek versions comes (contrary to (31) the usual rule) after the more accurate one. Perhaps the list denoted by ii. was perceived to be so grossly inaccurate that it was not allowed precedence, though the scribe of the Codex Vaticanus did not like to reject it altogether as the Codex Alexandrinus does.

* § 2. "*Darius*"[3]

Hitherto, the instances of name-conflation have been interesting chiefly as exemplifications of scribal error, and

---

[1] 1 S. xxi. 2 (Hebr. 3) פלני אלמני, Θεοῦ Πίστις, Φελλανεὶ Μαεμωνί.
[2] An anticipation of the eleventh name.
[3] For the meaning of the asterisk, see p. xix. n.

of the mental tendency to substitute the known for the unknown, and also of the general obscurity of Hebrew written without vowel-points; but none have risen to the level of a great historical error. Such an instance we now proceed to give.

[46] It relates to the Persian sovereigns who at first hindered and finally sanctioned that rebuilding of the Jewish temple which began in the first year of Cyrus king of Persia. The book of Ezra describes the Jews as coming up under Cyrus, and erecting the altar, and proceeding a little way with the building of the temple "in the second year of their coming unto the house of God at Jerusalem."[1] But at this point—

Ezra iv. 4-24 (R.V. (txt.))[2]: "The people of the land weakened the hands of the people of Judah, and troubled them in building, (5) and hired counsellors against them, to frustrate their purpose, all the days of Cyrus king of Persia, even until the reign of Darius king of Persia. (6) And in the reign of Ahasuerus, in the beginning of his reign, wrote they an accusation against the inhabitants of Judah and Jerusalem. (7) And in the days of Artaxerxes wrote Bishlam,[3] Mithredath . . . unto Artaxerxes. . . . [Here follows the letter to Artaxerxes, and his reply forbidding the erection of the temple.] (iv. 24) Then ceased the work of the house of God which is at Jerusalem, and it ceased unto the second year of the reign of Darius king of Persia."

[47] This is quite intelligible if Ahasuerus and Artaxerxes represent Persian sovereigns (preceding Darius), in

[1] Ezra iii. 8. Concerning the txt. of Ezr. iv. 6 f., see Adeney and Bennett's *Biblical Introduction*, p. 119, "The text is probably corrupt," *i.e.* the Hebrew and the Aramaic.

[2] Henceforth the Revised Version will usually be denoted, as here, by R.V. and the Authorised Version by A.V.

[3] But the LXX takes *B* as meaning "in" (which it does), and *shlm* as meaning "peace," and tells us that the letter was written "in peace."

whose reigns the building was in abeyance. We should then regard verses 6-23 as a long parenthesis (the Hebrew "and" in verse 6 being equivalent, as it often is, to "for" or "now") explaining the machinations by which the permission given by Cyrus was withdrawn and the temple brought to a stand.

But "Ahasuerus" is generally supposed to mean Xerxes the son of Darius, and Artaxerxes is supposed to be the son of Xerxes, and it is manifest that letters to the successors of Darius seem quite out of place here.

[48] Turning to the parallel statement in the first book of Esdras (ii. 16) we find no mention of Ahasuerus, but only of Artaxerxes as receiving this letter and as consequently forbidding the building.

The actual succession of Persian sovereigns was (i.) Cyrus; (ii.) his son Cambyses; (iii.) a pretender, Smerdis (who reigned but a few months); (iv.) Darius the son of Hystaspis, after whom followed Xerxes and then Artaxerxes.[1] But Cambyses is never mentioned; and Xerxes (if he is meant by Ahasuerus), together with Artaxerxes, seem mentioned out of place. The question arises whether the original Hebrew terms for any of these kings ("Cyrus," "Darius," "Ahasuerus," "Artaxerxes") are liable to be confused and whether they are actually confused.

[49] As regards actual confusion, we find that (i.) the Hebrew (or Aramaic) Daniel mentions a "Darius the Mede" of whom no trace has been found in history. (ii.) This "Darius the Mede" is described as conquering Babylon, whereas Cyrus was the real conqueror.[2] (iii.) The Hebrew Daniel implies, and the Septuagint expressly states, that "Cyrus received from [him]," *i.e.* succeeded to, the kingdom

---

[1] The eldest son of Xerxes was called Darius, presumably named thus after his grandfather Darius. But he was killed before ascending the throne, so that Artaxerxes succeeded Xerxes. The Greeks commonly named an eldest son after the grandfather. [2] Dan. v. 31.

of Darius.[1] (iv.) In one passage, both the Septuagint and Theodotion substitute "Cyrus" for the Hebrew "Darius."[2] (v.) In the first passage in which the Hebrew mentions "Darius the Mede," the Septuagint has "Artaxerxes the [?] of the Medes."[3] (vi.) A subsequent mention speaks of (Dan. ix. 1) "the first year of Darius the *son of Ahasuerus* (LXX, Xerxes) of the seed of the Medes," according to which this non-historical Darius has a father of the same name as the son (Xerxes) of the historical Darius.

[50] The possibilities of Hebrew corruption in (*a*) "Ahasuerus," and (*b*) "Artaxerxes" are in themselves considerable, as may be seen from some of the Greek attempts to transliterate them, *e.g.* (*a*) "Astheros," (*b*) "Asarthatha," "Astartha," etc., and from the fact that, in some texts of Esther, Ahasuerus is called by various forms of the name Artaxerxes.[4]

[51] But, further, both these words closely resemble another Persian word meaning "governor." It is transliterated in our Revised Version "Tirshatha," but the Septuagint represents it by forms still more like the names above-mentioned: Athersaa, Athersatha, Asersatha. And how easily Asersatha might be taken as a proper name appears from a passage in the first book of Esdras: "And *Naimias and Atharias* said unto them that they should not partake of the holy things"; where the parallel passage in Ezra has, "And *Athersaa* said unto them that they should not eat of the holy of holies"; and the Revised

---

[1] Dan. vi. 28: LXX, Κῦρος ὁ Πέρσης παρέλαβε τὴν βασιλείαν αὐτοῦ: Theod., as Hebr., "Daniel prospered in the reign of Darius and in the reign of Cyrus the Persian."

[2] Dan. xi. 1: "Darius the Mede"; LXX, "Cyrus the king"; Theod. "Cyrus."

[3] Dan. v. 31, Ἀρταξέρξης ὁ τῶν Μήδων. This would naturally mean "Artaxerxes, the [person of that name belonging to] the Medes." But there must be some error. See, however, 125.

[4] Black, *Ency. Bib.*, "Artaxerxes" and "Ahasuerus."

Version, "And the *Tirshatha* (marg. or, *governor*) said unto them."[1] It is obvious that this word might easily be taken to mean the governor of Babylon, or confused with the Hebrew equivalents of Artaxerxes and Xerxes.

[52] Now let us return to the passage in Ezra quoted at the beginning of this section about (*a*) plots in the days of Cyrus, (*b*) letters (authors unnamed) written "in the reign of Ahasuerus," and (*c*) letters from Bishlam and others "in the days of Artaxerxes." The first step to its elucidation is to examine the parallel passage in the First Book of Esdras. Doing this, we find that Esdras takes the passage to pieces and places two of the pieces at different stages of his narrative. Beginning with an appearance of logical order, he mentions (*c*) the letter from Bishlam[2] and his companions before its consequence—the stopping of the temple-building. Esdras says that it was written in the time of *Artaxerxes*. After giving the letter and the reply, he says that in consequence of the prohibition of Artaxerxes, building ceased till the second year of *Darius*.[3] Then comes a legendary account of Darius' permission to rebuild and then an account of the founding of the temple. And now, most inconsistently and preposterously, he places (*a*) the plotting during "all the days of the life of King *Cyrus*," and repeats a second time his statement about hindering till the reign of *Darius*, only in a corrupt form : "and they were hindered from building two years till the reign of Darius!"[4]

[53] Where is (*b*) the remaining piece (mentioning Ahasuerus)? Nowhere. Now, as a rule, Esdras conflates and amplifies, but does not omit anything that is given by Ezra. The absence of the name of Ahasuerus in Esdras, combined with the evidence of its confusion with Artaxerxes elsewhere, point to the conclusion that Esdras regarded the

---

[1] Ezra ii. 63=1 Esdr. v. 40. The LXX of parallel Neh. vii. 65 has "Asersatha," but אA "Athersatha."
[2] 1 Esdr. ii. 15 (16).   [3] *Ib.*, 30 (31).   [4] *Ib.*, v. 70 (73).

former as an erroneous repetition of the latter in a different shape. If that is the case, the passage quoted at the beginning of this section (Ezra iv. 4-6) is a Hebrew conflation. In any case we must conclude that great doubt attaches to all the Hebraic statements about Artaxerxes, Ahasuerus, and Darius the Mede.[1]

[54] It is even possible that the letters that stopped the building, if any letters were written at all, may have been written to, and by, Cyrus, or his representative at Babylon. Otherwise it must seem very extraordinary that a permission given by Cyrus in the first year of his Persian reign was abrogated during the rest of his reign without any countermand on his part. But if a countermand was issued by him, or by his representative, it might well happen that Jewish chroniclers would be unwilling to describe such a prohibition as coming from Cyrus, whom they regard as the Lord's instrument for good.[2] They would naturally prefer a vague term such as "the sovereign," using some Persian word. This might be subsequently defined, or rendered in translation, as "Xerxes" or "Artaxerxes."

§ 3. *Luke's misunderstanding about Herod Antipas*

[55] As compared with the translators of Ezra and Esdras, evangelists toward the end of the first century would have the advantage of being much nearer to the events they related: but they would also have a great disadvantage— the presence of a multitude of (i.) oral traditions, (ii.) written interpretations of the Hebrew *Logia*, (iii.) marginal comments on the latter in Hebrew (or sometimes Aramaic) or Greek. Hence it is impossible to accept without hesitation any important statement of fact made even by so painstaking

---

[1] As regards Darius some confusion may have been caused to Jewish writers by his being called "the son of Hystaspis."
[2] See *Ency. Bib.*, CYRUS, § 5.

a writer as Luke on his sole authority, if it appears that the other evangelists had no inducement at all to omit the fact, supposing they knew of it, and if the fact—supposing it to be a fact—was of very great interest to all Christians.

[56] These considerations apply to the statement, made by Luke alone, that Herod Antipas examined our Lord before the Crucifixion. A prophecy in Isaiah,[1] commonly regarded as Messianic, predicted that the Sufferer should be dumb "as a lamb that is led to the slaughter." All the other Evangelists represent Jesus (after the brief reply "Thou sayest") as "answering nothing" to *Pilate*. Luke alone refers this to *Herod*, thus :—

Mark xv. 5	Matth. xxvii. 14	Luke xxiii. 9
"But Jesus no longer answered anything, so that *Pilate* marvelled."	"And he answered him to never a word, so that *the governor* marvelled greatly."	"But he [Herod] questioned him with many words, but he made no answer to him."

Two hypotheses are almost equally incredible, (i.) that the earliest evangelists omitted this knowing it to be true; (ii.) that Luke inserted it knowing it to be false. We are led to consider a third hypothesis, (iii.) that Luke inserted it under a misunderstanding.

In the context, some words of Pilate are given by Mark thus, "Will ye that I release for you *the king of the Jews*?" by Matthew, "Whom will ye that *I release* for you, Barabbas or Jesus who is called Christ?" by Luke, "Having therefore chastised him I will *release* him." This indicates early divergence in the context of this tradition about "releasing." Now Luke never puts into Pilate's mouth the jesting application of "king" to Jesus. John emphasises it, using once the phrase, "*your* king."[2]

Suppose, then, an original tradition, "Pilate said to the

---
[1] Is. liii. 7.
[2] Mk. xv. 9, Mt. xxvii. 17, Lk. xxiii. 16 : "for you"=ὑμῖν : Jn. xix. 15.

Jews *that he would release Jesus their king.*" The Greek word used by Mark to mean "release" may also mean, and is used by Mark elsewhere to mean, "send away," and the Hebrew original might have the same double meaning.[1] Hence some interpreters—who perhaps thought it impossible that a Roman Governor should thus jest about a "king"—might easily render the tradition, either by Hebrew or by Greek corruption, "Pilate said to the Jews *that he would send away Jesus to their king.*" Now Herod Antipas, though only a tetrarch, might be called "king" for courtesy, and the adopters of this tradition might argue that Herod would naturally be in Jerusalem for the Passover, and that Pilate, when addressing a mingled crowd of Galilaean pilgrims and Jews, might style him thus, especially if he wished to pay him a compliment.[2] A marginal explanation might naturally be added to justify this novel interpretation, stating that Pilate remitted the accused to the tetrarch of Galilee because (as Luke states) he ascertained that Jesus was a Galilaean, under the jurisdiction of Antipas.

In order to do full justice to this hypothesis, we ought to compare other passages where Luke, with a perfectly honest intention, seems to have been led astray by mistranslation. This we are not as yet able to do. For the present, however, the reader may be fairly asked to keep an open mind on this story about Antipas, expecting to return to it again with the advantage of cumulative evidence on similar points. And perhaps, even now, some may feel that hypothesis (iii.) is at least more probable than (i.) or (ii.).

[57] No doubt, after Luke's tradition had originated from a corruption, or misunderstanding, of the text, it would be favoured and developed from controversial motives,

---

[1] Comp. Mk. viii. 9, ἀπέλυσεν αὐτούς, "he sent them away."

[2] Herod Antipas is called "king" in Mk. vi. 14 *f.*, Mt. xiv. 9. Luke would not probably in his own person call Antipas "king," but he might accept a tradition that Pilate called him "king" when he wanted to (Lk. xxiii. 12) conciliate the tetrarch.

because it fulfilled the Psalmist's words that "*kings* and rulers" should "take counsel together against the Lord and his Christ," and also because it shifted some of the blame from Pilate on to the Jewish prince. This last motive is apparent in the opening words of Pseudo-Peter:[1] "But of the Jews none washed his hands, neither Herod nor a single one of his *judges*." Here the phrase "his *judges*" may indicate the Hebrew origin of Luke's phrase "Herod and his *men of war*." The original may have been "men of *contention*," *i.e.* the *adversaries*, or *accusers*, of Jesus. The Hebrew word is rendered in Greek "battle" six times, "adversary" twice, "trial" six times, and "judgment" twenty-seven.[2] The indication of Hebraic origin shews the antiquity of Luke's misunderstanding.

[58] Very frequently indeed when Luke deviates from a passage of Mark in the Triple Tradition, it will be found that John steps in, throwing light on the deviation. Hence it is reasonable here to ask whether John has, in any shape, an account of Pilate's remission of the trial to a Governor of the Jews. There is none, of any actual remission; but John asserts that Pilate bade the chief priests take the accused and conduct the trial for themselves.

[59] Now in the Bible the title of "princes" or "rulers" is frequently applied in the Hebrew text to the chiefs of the priests, causing much perplexity to the Greek translators. For example, Chronicles speaks of "the *chiefs* (or princes) *of the priests* and the people" where the Septuagint has "the *nobles of Judah*, and *the priests*, and the people of the earth," and the parallel Esdras has "and moreover the rulers of the

---

[1] *The Gospel according to Peter*, § 1, οὐδὲ Ἡρώδης οὐδ' εἷς τῶν κριτῶν αὐτοῦ. The words come at the mutilated commencement of the Gospel, so that it is not clear to whom αὐτοῦ refers.

[2] Is. xli. 11, "adversaries," Heb. men of contention," ἀντίδικοι, Job xxxi. 35, κατά. In Jer. l. 34, li. 36, where the meaning is ("legal") cause," LXX has ἀντίδικος. See also Trommius on ריב. Luke's word, στρατεύματα, does not occur in Heb. LXX.

people and *of the priests*"; and where Ezra speaks of "the princes *of the priests*," the Septuagint has simply "rulers."[1]

[60] If therefore some tradition was current in the Christian Church at Jerusalem that "Pilate gave command to send Jesus for trial to the *Prince of the priests* and to the men of contention," and if this was taken to mean "*a Prince of the Jewish people* and his men of war," this would suggest another way of explaining Luke's story.

The possibility of applying reasoning deducible from Septuagint name-conflations to passages in the Gospels, may be confirmed by facts relating to the only cure of blindness recorded by all the Synoptists, which will be the subject of the next section.

§ 4. "*The Son of Timaeus, Bartimaeus*"[2]

[61] This name is recorded by Mark alone. "Bar-" means "son of." Hence "the son of Timaeus" and "Bartimaeus" mean the same thing. But Mark puts the two words together, as though they were two Greek names. Elsewhere, when he gives the interpretation of an Aramaic appellation, he says "Boanerges, *which is*, Sons of thunder"; and Luke says, "Barnabas, *which is*, Son of consolation." But here the usual phrase denoting interpretation is omitted. Moreover, the order here is strange. We should expect, as in the two passages just quoted, that the Aramaic would come *first*, and the interpretation *second*, "Bar-timaeus, which is, Son of Timaeus."

[62] Suspicion is also thrown on the name by four facts. (i.) It is rejected by all the later Gospels. (ii.) Matthew mentions *two* blind men, which suggests that he had before

---

[1] 2 Chr. xxxvi. 14 "chiefs of (שׂרי)"; LXX, οἱ ἔνδοξοι Ἰούδα καὶ οἱ ἱερεῖς καὶ ὁ λαὸς τῆς γῆς. . . ., 1 Esdr. i. 47, καὶ οἱ ἡγούμενοι δὲ τοῦ λαοῦ καὶ τῶν ἱερέων. Comp. Ezra x. 5: "the chiefs of the priests;" LXX simply ἄρχοντας, but parall. 1 Esdr. viii. 92 φυλάρχους τῶν ἱερέων.

[2] Mk. x. 46, Mt. xx. 30, Lk. xviii. 35. "Bar-" is late Hebrew and Aramaic for "son of." It is very rare in O.T. The usual form is "Ben-".

him some tradition that so far agreed with Mark as to recognise *two names*, but did not venture to give them as authoritative. (iii.) The Sinaitic Syrian and the Arabic Diatessaron agree with the Peshitta in reading " Timai the son of Timai." (iv.) Timaeus is an ancient Greek name, meaning "honourable." But Greek words are rarely, if ever, found after the Aramaic prefix " Bar-." We find Bar-nabas, Bar-jona, Bar-sabas, Bar-jesus, Bar-abbas—but never such an apparent hybrid as this. This last fact might indeed be used as an argument for the genuineness of the name : " If Mark had invented it, would he have gone out of his way to invent a hybrid ? " Certainly not, but he may have created an *apparent* hybrid, by transliterating a Hebrew gloss so as to produce an impossible name.

[63] Before going further, we may remark that such an argument as " the author would not have *invented* the name " often falls to the ground in the face of even a very slight amount of evidence showing that the name *may have sprung from a gloss.*

For example, the *Acta Sanctorum* commemorates the martyrdom of the soldier who pierced Christ's side with a " spear." John calls the spear " lonché," and the " soldier " is appropriately called " Longinus," which happens to be a Latin name. Everyone can see how easily a Latin marginal gloss may have originated this, and few students would hesitate to accept this explanation. Similarly, too, perhaps, may be explained the very early name " Dysmas," applied to the penitent malefactor who was on the right hand of the Cross. The word is a transliteration of the Greek term for " sunset " or " west," and if the Cross faced the south, the Latin Church may have welcomed the symbolical suggestion that the West repented while the East remained impenitent.[1]

[1] This, if we could similarly explain the name of the impenitent malefactor "Gistas" (or "Gestas"), might be regarded as almost certain. At present it has only a fair probability.

The earliest mention of Dysmas is in the text of the *Acta Pilati*, and perhaps the earliest mention of Longinus is in a MS. of that work, but no one accuses the author, or the scribe, of "inventing." The names *grew*.

[64] It remains to shew that names could "*grow*" in the same way in the Bible. Above (42), only one such instance was given. But here are others:[1]

(*a*) 1 Chr. xxv. 4-5, tells us that "God gave to Heman fourteen sons and three daughters," and prefixes the names of the sons. But some of them, "at least the last six," are fashioned out of "a prayer or meditation." Instead of "Hananiah, Hanani, Eliathah, etc.," we are to read, "Be gracious to me, Jah, Be gracious to me, thou art my God," and so on.

(*b*) 1 Chr. iv. 21. "Jashubi-lehem" has arisen from a misunderstanding of the text, "And they returned to Bethlehem."

(*c*) 1 Chr. ii. 25*f.* "Ahijah", is probably "to be struck out, having arisen from an original misinterpretation of 'his brother.'"

(*d*) 1 Chr. iii. 17, 18. "Assir," as a proper name, "arose from a misunderstanding of the adj. *assir* meaning captive."

(*e*) 1 Chr. viii. 13*f.* "Ahio" is "certainly to be rejected," being, like (*c*), a confusion of "brother."

(*f*) 1 Chr. viii. 44. "Bocheru" should be read as "his first-born" (the unpointed consonants being capable of either interpretation).

(*g*) 1 Chr. xxiv. 26 and 27. "Beno," which occurs twice as a proper name, means "his son." In the first case, whereas LXX omits it, A conflates it as "Sons of *Beno*"![2]

[65] The preceding instances are taken from the Old

---

[1] See Hastings' *Dict. Bib.* vol. ii. pp. (*a*) 124, (*b*) 126, (*c*) 126, (*d*) 127, (*e*) 131, (*f*) 131, (*g*) 125.

[2] To these may be added 1 K. iv. 8. "Ben-hur," Βαιώρ (A, Βεν υιος ωρ, *i.e.* "Ben, son of Hor").

Testament. We shall now adduce one from the New—the insertion by Mark of a name that is omitted by Matthew and Luke, and that is contrary to historical facts.

Mk. ii. 25-26. "Have ye never read what David did ... how he entered into the house of God *when Abiathar was high priest*." Turning to the history we find, "Then came David to Nob to *Ahimelech* the priest, and *Ahimelech* came to meet him ..." and it is then said that Ahimelech gave David some of the shew-bread.[1] No one denies that Ahimelech, not Abiathar, was "the priest" in question, so that Mark has apparently assigned a mis-statement to Christ.[2] Even those who—in spite of Matthew's and Luke's omission of the name—accept unhesitatingly the authenticity of "the son of Timaeus, Bartimaeus," hesitate about, or reject, the statement that "Abiathar was high priest" at the time in question.

The solution of the difficulty is probably to be found in the similarity, in Hebrew, between (i.) "*to the house of* the priest"; and (ii.), "*Abiathar* the priest,"[3] the former being the correct rendering of the original. Later interpreters took "the house," to mean (iii.) "the House of God," as it often does;[4] and this, in Matthew and Luke, supplanted (i.). Mark *added* (iii.) to his text. Then, since "To the House of God *to the house of* the priest," made no sense, it was natural to adopt a gloss interpreting "to the house of," as "Abiathar"—the particular high priest whose name is most frequently associated with that of David.[5]

---

[1] 1 S. xxi. 1-6.

[2] Few competent judges would accept, as an explanation, so forced a rendering as "in the presence of Abiathar [afterwards] high priest." Professor Swete says "the clause is peculiar to Mark and may be an editorial note."

[3] "To the house of"=אלבית (or על for אל as in 1 S. ii. 11 quoted below), "Abiathar"=אביתר.

[4] *Hor. Hebr.* i. 64-5, says that the Court of the Gentiles was called "the Mountain of *the House*," *i.e.*, the Temple.

[5] In 1 S. ii. 11 "He went *to his* (Elkanah's) *house* (עלביתו)" is omitted by

[66] Returning now to "the son of Timaeus, Bartimaeus," we are justified by the evidence of name-errors in the Old Testament (and apparently in Mark's own Gospel), by the difficulties inherent in the name, and by the deviations of early versions, in attaching much more weight than before to the non-insertion of the names in Matthew and Luke, and to the fact that Matthew mentions two persons instead of one. But, proceeding by analogy, we shall not be justified in saying that Mark "invented" the name. The right question to ask is, "*What kind of gloss could have originated the name?*"

This question appears to be met by the fact that "Bartimaeus" is represented as a "beggar," and that, in the only instances in which the word "beg" occurs in the Bible, it is implied that begging is a degradation reserved for the children of *sinners*: "I have been young and now am old, yet have I not seen the righteous forsaken nor his seed *begging* their bread": "Let his (*i.e.*, the sinner's) children be vagabonds and *beg*."[1] That "sinners," in such a case, might be called "the unclean" is indicated by the *Horae Hebraicae*: "It was a received doctrine in the Jewish schools, that children, according to some wickedness of their parents, were born lame, or crooked ... by which they kept parents in awe, lest they should grow remiss and negligent in the performance *of such rites which had respect to their being clean, such as washings, purifyings*, etc."[2] Accordingly, in the case of the man born blind, described by John—concerning whom the disciples ask whether he or his parents had sinned—when we find the Pharisees saying to the afflicted man, "Thou wast altogether *born in sin*," it appears that they may have *included parental "uncleanness" in their imputation of sin.*

LXX, which inserts "before the Lord." Is the latter based on a rendering of "his house," as "His House," *i.e.*, the House of God? If so, A, which adds "to their house," has a conflation.

[1] Ps. xxxvii. 25, cix. 10. Comp. Sir. xl. 28. "Better it is to die than to beg."
[2] *Hor. Hebr.*, on Jn. ix. 2, and comp. *ib.* on Mk. vii. 4.

CONFLATIONS OF NAMES

[67] We have been led, then, step by step, to the conclusion that the name "Bartimaeus" is an editorial addition derived from some marginal gloss, and that it may have referred to some parental "sin" or "uncleanness." If we can find no such reference latent in "Bartimaeus," the conclusion must remain a mere reasonable conjecture, but if we can find one, the probability of the conclusion will be greatly increased.

The reader will perhaps be surprised to hear that the most natural Hebrew root from which "Timaeus" could have been obtained by transliteration is the Old Testament word in regular use to denote "unclean." "Why," he may ask, "did not commentators suggest this origin?" The answer is that probably many of them assumed that Bartimaeus must be "well known in the times of the Apostles," and perhaps were also induced by the Greek meaning of Timaeus to suppose that it had a favourable meaning.[1] How could a man who was "well known" or "famous" in the days of the Apostles bear a name that meant "son of the unclean?" But those who approach the discussion of the name with no prejudice in favour of its being a name of honourable signification, and with minds open to believe that Mark may have been led astray here by a gloss, as he appears to have been in the case of Abiathar, will be prepared by the above-mentioned considerations to accept as highly probable the conclusion that the name sprang from an early Jewish gloss stating that this afflicted man had been called by the Pharisees "son of the unclean."

---

[1] *Hor. Hebr.* suggests "son of *admiration* (תימה)," "son of *profit* (טימי)," or "son of one *blind* " (טימא) being used for (טימא). Victor, quoted by Prof. Swete *ad loc.*, says, ὀνομαστὶ δεδήλωκεν ὁ Μᾶρκος . . . ὡς ἐπιφανῆ τότε ὄντα, a word that means "famous," "illustrious," more often than "well-known." Prof. Swete himself says "Βαρτιμαῖος . . . is clearly a patronymic analogous to Βαρθολομαῖος, =(?) בר מְמָאִי." The letters טמא mean nothing but "unclean," "defiled," etc., in O.T. But Prof. Swete does not draw any inference from the letters. He says, " Bengel is doubtless right in saying: 'notus Apostolorum tempore Bartimaeus.' "

[68] On this supposition, the omission of the words of interpretation ("which is"), the silence of Luke, the mention of "two blind men" in Matthew, and the various reading "Timai the son of Timai," are all explicable. We cannot indeed feel sure whether the original gloss was simply "Timai," or "Timai the son of Timai." But in either case, (i.) the transference of the gloss into the text explains why Mark omits the usual words of interpretation; (ii.) doubt about the authenticity of the gloss might lead Matthew to reject the two *names* while inferring that there were two *persons;* (iii.) conviction that it was non-authentic would lead Luke to omit it altogether.[1]

This conviction, whether it was Luke's or not, may very well commend itself to careful and dispassionate students of the New Testament.

[1] As an illustration of the use of "Timai" (apart from vowel points) we may quote the enactment about the leper, Lev. xiii. 45-46, "He shall cry, *Unclean, Unclean* (טמא טמא)," where the LXX has "he shall *be called unclean.*" In conclusion it should be noted that Matthew omits mention of "begging." This may have been caused, not by a desire to suppress the fact, but from a confusion between "asking" for bread, and "asking" for pity. Luke alone inserts that the man "*inquired* who it was." This may be another version of the "asking" (*i.e.* "begging").

CHAPTER IV

CONFLATIONS OF TECHNICAL TERMS, DATES, ETC.

§ 1. *Technical terms*

TECHNICAL terms, since they approach the nature of names, are almost equally liable to conflation, of which the following are instances :—

[69] 1 S. x. 5 : (lit.) "Where [there] *the garrison of* the Philistines is," LXX "Where is there the (a_1) *erection* of the foreigners, there (a_2) *Naseib* the foreigner." [1] Here "garrison" is first translated "erection" and then transliterated. *The twofold translation of one word causes the repetition of the context.* This often happens on a much larger scale.

2 K. ix. 13 : "On the *top of* (*grm*) the stairs," LXX "On the *garem* of the stairs." Codex *A*, by Greek corruption, reads "gar ena," *i.e.* "*for one* of the steps." The version of Lucianus conflates thus, " on (a_1) *one* (neut.) of the (a_2) *garem* on (a_3) *one* (fem.) of the steps." [2]

[70] Josh. v. 10 : "At even, in *the plains of* (*a″rbth*) Jericho," LXX "from the evening, (a_1) *from the west of* Jericho, (a_2) on the *other side of Jordan*, (a_3) in *the plain.*"

The "Arabah" was the technical name given to the low-lying country about Jericho and the Dead Sea, the southern valley of the Jordan. The Hebrew here is "Araboth," the

---

[1] 1 S. x. 5, "where"=in Heb. the indecl. rel. followed by "there," lit. "which there." This perplexes the LXX. " Foreigners (ἀλλόφυλοι) " is the regular rendering of "Philistines." " Garrison-of "=נצב.

[2] Codex *A*. γαρ ενα. R.V. marg. has "the *bare* stairs."

plural of "Arabah." Aquila frequently renders it "the level." But the root also means "evening" and "west."[1] Again, $a''rb$ is sometimes confused with $a''br$ meaning "on the other side of." The LXX is influenced by these possibilities. It introduces "Jordan" from a vague feeling that this is implied by the term "Arabah." But again "*on the other side of* Jordan" is a familiar phrase, and a slight transposition in the word for "west" converts it into "on the other side." The result is a triple conflation of two inaccurate translations with one accurate one, which comes last.[2]

[71] A very similar introduction of "Jordan" occurs in Matthew's and Luke's accounts of John the Baptist. Mark mentions "the men of Jerusalem and the country of Judaea," meaning "the country" as distinct from "the capital city" of Judaea, or, in other words, the country *round about the city*. For clearness, "country" was probably changed to "country-round-about." But this term is habitually connected, in Genesis, with "Jordan." Matthew and Luke adopt "the-surrounding-country of Jordan."[3]

[72] 2 S. xix. 18: "And *there-went-across* ($a''br$) the *ferry-boat* ($a''br$, lit. *crossing*) to *bring-across* ($a''br$) the king's household"; LXX, "(A₁) and they *ministered* ($a''bd$) *the ministration* ($a''bd$) to *bring-across* the king, (A₂) and *there-went across* the *going-across* to stir up the house of the king."

The confusion of the Hebrew r and d—shewn (**5-8**) to be of constant occurrence—here causes "go across ($a''br$)"

---

[1] [70*a*] Josh. v. 10: LXX, "From the west (ἀπὸ δυσμῶν)." Δυσμαί, when = מערב, is "westward" (as in 1 Chr. vii. 28); when = ערבה, it is "plain," as in Num. xxii. 1, xxxiii. 48.

[2] The LXX may have been further confused by the fact that the word $a''rb$ occurs in the context in its usual sense of "evening."

[3] Mk. i. 5, Mt. iii. 5, Lk. iii. 3. Comp. Jn. xi. 55: "Out of *the country*," *i.e.* the country round about Jerusalem. Περίχωρος is connected with "Jordan" in Gen. xiii. 10, 11, and is used absolutely to mean "the circle of the Jordan," in Gen. xiii. 17, 28.

to be confused in A_1 with "minister ($a''bd$)." In A_2, this error is corrected, though a new one is introduced.[1]

[73] This passage may have a bearing on one in Mark where Jesus is said to have ordered that a boat should be "in attendance" on Him. The two words "boat" and "attend" may there, as here, be a conflation.[2] Matthew and Luke omit all reference to the boat. Elsewhere (171) Mark and Matthew mention a "boat" but Luke omits it.

[74] Ex. xxi. 6 : "Then his master shall bring him unto *God* (*Elohim*)," (R.V. marg. and A.V., "the judges "); LXX, "(a_1) the *judgment-place* (a_2) of *God*," conflating the usual with the unusual meaning of *Elohim*.

[75] 2 S. xv. 18 (lit. Heb.) : "And all his servants passed on at his hand, and all the Cherethites, and all the Pelethites, and all the Gittites, six hundred men, who came at his feet (*i.e.* after him) from Gath, passed on before the king."

The translators were perplexed partly by the titles of David's bodyguard, partly by other confusions of which the explanation would be too lengthy. The result is the following triple conflation in the LXX.

The first (a_1) confuses "the Gittites" and "six hundred men," and also "Gath."

The second (a_2), which is of the nature of a free non-Hebraic paraphrase, translates the titles of the warriors, and gives their number correctly, but omits "the Gittites" and "Gath."

The third (a_3) is the most correct and complete, but mistakes "*at* his feet" for "*with* their feet," and makes the men come "to" Gath instead of "from" it.[3] The ultimate combination is as follows, literally translated :—"(a_1) And all

---

[1] "Stir up "=hiph. of עור, which the LXX, in A_2, has erroneously substituted for עבר. Conflated *sentences*, as distinct from conflated *words*, will be denoted by A_1, A_2, instead of a_1, a_2.

[2] Mk. iii. 9, ἵνα πλοιάριον προσκαρτερῇ αὐτῷ.

[3] [75a] See 335b, comparing Luke's statement that John came *to* "the surrounding country of the Jordan," with Matthew's that men came *from* it to John.

his servants at his hand passed by, and all Chettei and all the Phelethei,[1] and halted at the olive tree in the wilderness and all the people went by close to him; (a_2) and all those about him and all the valiant and all the warriors six hundred men; (a_3) and there were by him at his hand both all the Chereththei (*sic*) and all the Pheleththei and all the Geththaeans the six hundred men the [men] that came on their feet to Gath and going before the face of the king."

[76] It will be noted that *not one of these conflations translates "at his feet" (i.e. "following him") correctly*. Both here and in the context the phrase is translated "*on foot*," or "*with* their feet."[2] A similar error, resulting in conflation, almost certainly exists in Matthew as compared with Mark and Luke:—

Mark vi. 33	Matt. xiv. 13	Luke ix. 11
"(a_2) *on foot* from all the cities."	"(a_1) *followed him* (a_2) *on foot* from the cities."	"(a_1) *followed him*."

§ 2. *Conflations of dates*

There are several passages in the Synoptic Gospels that contain perplexing mentions of time or date. Hence importance attaches to the following conflations:—

[77] Dan. ix. 26 (lit.): "After weeks sixty and two." So, too, Theodotion. But the Hebrew "week" (like the old English "se'nnight," *i.e.* "seven night") resembles the Hebrew "seven," and also the Hebrew "seventy." Hence the LXX has "after (a_1) *seven* and (a_2) *seventy*, and sixty-two."

[78] Ezra iv. 24: (lit.) "And it [*i.e.* the building of the Temple] ceased *until the year two* (R.V. *second*) [belonging]

---

[1] Πᾶς Χεττεὶ καὶ πᾶς ὁ Φελεθεί.
[2] 2 S. xv. 16-18: "At his feet (Hebr. ברגליו and ברגלו)," τοῖς ποσὶν αὐτῶν (twice), and πεζῇ (once).

to the reign [*i.e.* of the reign] of Darius king of Persia. Now the prophets, Haggai. . . ." This is parallel to—

1 Esdr. v. 70 (R.V. 73): "And they were kept from building (a_1) *two years until* the reign of Darius. But (a_2) *in the second year* of the reign of Darius there prophesied Haggai. . . ." The Aramaic word here translated in Ezra (R.V.) "second" is rendered "two" by Theodotion in Daniel.[1] From these facts follows a conclusion, to which we shall have hereafter to refer, that ordinal and cardinal numbers may be confused in the process of translation from Hebrew. See **226**.

[79] Gen. viii. 5: "Until the tenth month. In the tenth [month] on the first of the month"; LXX, "until the tenth month; but (a_1) in the *eleventh* month, (a_2) on *the first* of the month." The translator rendered "tenth first" as (a_1) "eleventh."[2] The corrector placed (a_2) "on the first" in the margin. The copyist or editor conflated the two.

[80] Ezra iii. 8 (lit.): "Now in the second year *to* [*i.e.* of] their coming into the house of God, in the second month" LXX, "in the second year of their coming." This is correct. But it is parallel to—

1 Esdr. v. 54 (56)-55 (57) (lit.): (a_1) "*And having come in the second year* to the temple of God . . . (a_2) on the day of the new moon of the second month of *the second year in their coming* [*i.e.* after they had come] to Judaea and Jerusalem." Here a_1 is an error, and a_2 is a correct translation made more logical than the original Hebrew. For the translator reflects that, as the Temple was not yet in existence, but only on the point of being built, the Jews could not well be

---

[1] Dan. v. 31: "two (תרין)," Theod. δύο (LXX paraphrases). In numbering days of the month and years the forms of the cardinals are regularly used in Hebrew.

[2] Comp. Mt. x. 29, Lk. xii. 6, where the original was possibly "two [or] three sparrows for a farthing," and Luke may have followed a tradition corrupting the regular Hebraic idiom "two [or] three" into "five" with other consequent modifications. See below (**225**).

said to "come to the house of God." The writer of a_1 alters (as often elsewhere) "*house* of God" to "*temple*," an expression more familiar to Greeks; the writer of a_2 substitutes "Judaea and Jerusalem."

§ 3. *The hour of the Crucifixion*

These facts may be applied to the well-known apparent discrepancy in the Gospels as to the hour of the Crucifixion.
[81] (i.) Mark says, "Now it was the third hour and they crucified him." (ii.) John, immediately before describing how Pilate delivered Jesus to be crucified, says, "it was about the sixth hour." (iii.) The synoptists agree that from the sixth hour to the ninth hour there was darkness over the whole land. (iv.) Mark and Matthew state, and Luke implies, that Jesus died at the ninth hour.[1]

[82] On the hypothesis of translation from the Hebrew, all these statements can be reconciled, if we regard Mark's statement about "the third hour" as being a marginal addition inserted out of place, and "*the third* hour *and*" as a mistranslation of "*three hours since*" (just as (**78**), in Esdras,[2] "*second* year" is confused with "*two* years").

[83] Let us suppose that, in the Original, this marginal clause was intended to come after the description of the darkness and immediately before the description of Christ's death, thus: "And as soon as the sixth hour had come there had come darkness over the whole land [and it lasted] until the ninth hour—*it being now three hours since* they had crucified him—and at the ninth hour Jesus cried out."[3]

---

[1] Mk. xv. 25, ἦν δὲ ὥρα τρίτη καὶ ἐσταύρωσαν αὐτόν: Jn. xix. 14, ὥρα ἦν ὡς ἕκτη. Mk. xv. 34, καὶ τῇ ἐνάτῃ ὥρᾳ ἐβόησεν: Mt. xxvii. 46, περὶ δὲ τὴν ἐνάτην ὥραν ἐβόησεν, Lk. om.

[2] For convenience, "the first book of Esdras" will be called simply "Esdras."

[3] [83*a*] "As soon as the sixth hour *had come* (γενομένης) ... *there had come* (ἐγένετο). ..." The pluperfect in Hebrew is non-existent. But it is a frequent habit in Hebrew writing to go back to the past with a supplementary clause that

According to this hypothesis, the clause originally *assumed* that Jesus had been crucified about the sixth hour, and explained "from the sixth to the ninth" by saying that this was the interval ("three hours") that had elapsed between the crucifixion and the "loud cry" and death, which are now to be described. But "since" was confused with "when," and, as in Esdras, the cardinal number was taken as an ordinal. Thus the words were converted into a statement about *the time when the crucifixion took place*, and, in this shape, the marginal clause, instead of being inserted in its right place, was transposed to an earlier position where the crucifixion was described. Indeed such a transposition may well have happened even if the mistranslated clause was a part of the text of the original Hebrew Gospel.[1] Thus we can explain Matthew's and Luke's omission of the phrase and John's correction of it.[2]

implies a pluperfect. This, in theory, ought to be expressed by a Greek pluperfect; but, owing to the disuse of this tense, the LXX mostly prefers the aorist. (241a).

[1] [83b] Comp. Mk. xii. 12, Mt. xxii. 22, "and they left him, and went away, (καὶ ἀφέντες αὐτὸν ἀπῆλθον), placed by Mark before, but by Matthew after, the dialogue with the Pharisees and Herodians about tribute.

[2] [83c] Even without the hypothesis of transposition, the view advocated above might hold good on the supposition that the original author of Mark intended his readers to connect Mk. xv. 25 with xv. 33, thus: "(25) And it was now three hours from the time of his being crucified. . . . (33) And as soon as the sixth hour [the hour of the crucifixion] had come, darkness had come over the whole land, lasting till the ninth hour. (34) And at the ninth hour Jesus called aloud." The description of the inscription, the malefactors, and the mocking (xv. 26-32) may have been intended to be taken parenthetically.

CHAPTER V

OTHER TYPICAL CONFLATIONS

* § 1. *Variations of grammatical form*[1]

IN the following instances, conflation has arisen from translating one word as having two grammatical forms, *e.g.* a verb as past and future, active and passive, etc.

[**84**] 2 Chr. xxv. 18 (lit.) : "And there passed by a beast of the field that was in Lebanon and trod down"; LXX, "(a_1) And behold *there shall come* the beasts of the field in Lebanon, (a_2) and *there came* the beasts and trod down."

[**85**] 1 K. xviii. 43 : "*Go-again* (lit. (re)turn) seven times"; LXX, "(a_1) *Return* seven times, (a_2) and *turn away* seven times, (a_3) and the servant *turned away* seven times." The Hebrew " go-again," literally " (re)turn," produces a threefold conflation.

[**86**] The change of tense adds a third variation, illustrating once more the important rule that (**28**) *in translating from Hebrew, commands may be corrupted into statements of fact and vice versa.* See **240**.

[**87**] In Josh. viii. 18, the LXX inserts "and the liers in wait *shall speedily rise up* from their place," anticipating what is subsequently expressed in the past tense, Josh. viii. 19, "and the liers in wait *rose up* out of their place." The former is not in the Hebrew.

[**88**] Ezek. xii. 12 : "He shall not see with his eyes the

[1] For the meaning of *, see p. xix. n.

ground"; LXX, "(a_1) *lest he* [or *it*] *should be seen* with the eye, (a_2) *and he* (emph. form) *shall not see* the ground."

[89] Job xxxvii. 20 (lit. Hebr.): "Shall it be recounted"; LXX, "(a_1) *Book* or (a_2) *scribe.*" The passive verb is taken as (a_1) "written account," *i.e.* "book," (a_2) "one that writes an account," *i.e.* "scribe."

[90] Conflations illustrating the most common kind of confusions of letters—*e.g.* between *d* and *r*—are of importance, and especially those which bear on suspected mistranslations in the Gospel, *e.g.* Matthew's use of "companion" where we might expect "thou wicked one."[1]

Prov. vi. 3 : "Into the hands of thy *neighbour*"; LXX, "(a_1) Into the hands of *the wicked* (a_2) for the sake of *thy friend.*"

Eccles. vii. 22 : "Oftentimes thine own heart *knoweth*"; LXX, "(a_1) oftentimes it will *work evil* on thee (a_2) and on many occasions thy heart will *do mischief.*" This is a rather unusual instance, a conflation of two translations having similar meanings, and both of them wrong. ["Thy heart," "thy soul," etc., often mean "thyself" in Hebrew.] For other instances, see **7**.

[91] Even a familiar name may sometimes cause confusion when used in an unfamiliar phrase, *e.g.* "in David," which occurs in a dispute between the men of Israel and the men of Judah. The phrase somewhat resembles the word "first-born,"[2] which seemed an appropriate epithet for the former to claim. Hence the following conflation in :—

2 S. xix. 43 : (lit.) "And also *in David* I more than thou," *i.e.*, as R.V., "We have also more [right] in David than ye"; LXX "(a_1) And *first-born* I than thou, (a_2) and certainly *in David* I am above thee."

[92] The distinction between *sh* and *s* is absent alto-

---

[1] "Companion" and "bad" both = רע; "know" (imperat.) = רע. For Matthew's use of "companion," see below (**188**).

[2] "In David (ברוד)," "first-born (בכור)."

gether when the Hebrew consonant is left unpointed. Hence *the word " elders-of (sbi)," when it occurs in Ezra, is regularly translated " captivity (shbi) " in Esdras.* In the following instance, Esdras conflates the two meanings. The reader should also note how the Hellenizing Esdras avoids the anthropomorphic expression " the eye of God " :—

Ezra v. 5 : " The eye of their God was upon *the elders of the Jews.*" 1 Esdr. vi. 5 : " Favour was found, through the visitation of God, (a_1) *on the captivity* of the Jews, (a_2) *by the elders of* the Jews." [1]

[93] A similar confusion, with the dropping of a letter, explains 2 Chr. xxxv. 15, " the porters," rightly translated in the parallel 1 Esdr. i. 15 (R.V. 16), " the *porters*," but conflated by the LXX in Chronicles, " (a_1) the *rulers* (a_2) and the *porters*." [2]

Bearing in mind that " gates " (as in " within *thy gates* ") often means " cities," we find precisely the same error in Judg. v. 8, " gates," LXX (a_1) " *cities* (a_2) of *rulers.*"

[94] Owing to the similarity between the preposition " for " and " not," the particle " therefore " (" for-this ") is very frequently rendered " not thus." [3] In the following parallel passages, the translator of Kings wedges another error (" not I ") between two instances of an erroneously translated " therefore " :—

1 K. xxii. 19 (2 Chr. xviii. 18) : " *Therefore* hear thou (Chr. ye) the word of the Lord " ; LXX (K.), " (a_1) *Not thus ;* (a_2) *not I ;* hear thou the word of the Lord ; (a_3) *not thus.*" Chronicles is content with a single translation, but an erroneous one, " *Not thus ;* hear ye the word of the Lord."

---

[1] " Elders of (שׂבי)," " captivity (of) (שׁבי)." In 1 Esdr. vi. 5, read γενομένης with A.   [2] " Porters (שׁערים)."   " Rulers "=שׂרים.

[3] [94a] " Not thus "=לאכן (sometimes written as two words), but לא is sometimes written לו. " Therefore "=לכן. The last three letters of " not thus " are the same (though not in the same order) as the first three letters of " I (אנכי)."

* § 2. *Longer conflations*

[95] The same ignorance or carelessness that leads a translator to confuse one word in a sentence may naturally lead him to confuse another. Moreover, a first error often suggests a second as "necessary for the sense." Hence some passages exhibit a group of conflations so complicated as to make it rather difficult to associate them with a Hebrew original even when we have the latter before us.

2 S. xv. 34 : (lit.) "Thy servant, I, O king, will be. Servant of thy father as I (lit. and I) hitherto [have been], so now also (lit. and now) so I (lit. and I) thy servant [will be]." This means (R.V.) "I will be thy servant, O king. As I have been thy father's servant in time past, so will I now be thy servant." But the ambiguity of the Hebrew conjunctions, the omission of verbs, and some confusions of letters, lead the Septuagint to the following result :—"(a_1) Thy brethren have *passed across*, and the king behind me has *passed across* thy father (*nom.*). And now thy *servant* I am, O king ; (a_2) suffer me to live, *servant* of thy father I was then and lately, and now I [am] thy servant."

[96] At first sight it seems hopeless to attempt to explain this. But proceeding step by step, we could go some way towards the truth, even though there were no Hebrew. For we should decide, first, that if this was an instance of conflation (31) *the substance of the original would probably be found at the end.* That rule would lead us to say, in this particular case, "There must have been something about *servants* in the original." In the next place, knowing from repeated experience that "across" ($a''br$) is liable to confusions, and that r is confused with d, and knowing that $a''bd$ means "servant," we perceive that "pass across," in a_1, represents "servant." Further examination

shews that "brethren" is an error for "I" and "behind me" for "(I) will be."[1]

[97] It sometimes happens that the first member of a conflation, though paraphrastic or grammatically incorrect, is substantially right, while the second member, though more literal, in the attempt to remedy the grammatical incorrectness, falls into a far worse error. Thus, where the Gibeonites say that Saul "devised we shall be destroyed," the Septuagint first paraphrases this, making "he" the subject, "devised that *he* should destroy *us*"; and then, reverting to the Hebrew so far as to make "we" the subject, gives "that *we* should destroy *him*." Besides the grammatical conflation, the two verbs "consume" and "destroy" are also conflated:—

2 S. xxi. 5 : "The man that[2] (*a*) *consumed* us, and that devised against us [that] we should be [marg. so that we have been] (*b*) *destroyed*"; LXX, "The man (a_1) *consummated* against us and (a_2) *persecuted* us, [the man] that devised (b_1) to *destroy us* (b_2) let *us exterminate him*."

So, too, Josh. i. 8 : "Thou shalt make thy way prosperous"; LXX, "(a_1) Thou *shalt be prospered*, and (a_2) he *shall prosper thy ways*." Here (a_1) was substantially correct, though it omitted "ways," which would be superfluous in Greek, and against Greek usage. The author of (a_2), while restoring the Hebraic "ways," has changed "thou," which was correct, into "he."

[98] In the following instance from Esdras, the first place is given to an attempt at a literal translation with amplification, and the second to a brief summary. The original is in Ezra vi. 20 : (lit.) "For there had purified

---

[1] [96*a*] (i.) "Servant (עבד)," LXX διέρχεσθαι (*bis*) (*leg.* עבר). (ii.) "I (אני)," LXX οἱ ἀδελφοί σου (*leg.* אחיך). (iii.) "I will be (אהיה)," κατόπισθέν μου (*leg.* אחרי). (iv.) Ἔασόν με ζῆσαι (suffer me to live)," probably arose from taking "let me be (אהיה)" as "let me live (אחיה)."

[2] 2 S. xxi. 5 : "The man (איש) that (אשר)"; LXX omits "that," perhaps confusing איש with אשר.

themselves [A.V. " were purified "] the priests and the Levites as-one, all-of-them pure." In Esdras there is a twofold conflation, in which a_1 translates the Hebrew conjunction " for " as " when," which it often means. It also takes " all " as meaning " the whole people," and to express this it adds " the children of the captivity." Perhaps " for " was inserted in the margin as an alternative for " when "; at all events, it adds, at the end of a_1, "*for* they were purified." Then follows a_2, a condensed translation of the whole, beginning with " for." The total result is (1 Esdr. vii. 10-11): "(a_1) *When* there were purified the priests and the Levites together and all the sons of the captivity, *for* they were purified; (a_2) *for* the Levites together all were purified."

The Septuagint version of Ezra renders briefly and closely thus, "*Because* there were purified the priests and the Levites as one[1] all pure."

[99] In the following conflation, A_2 inserts the important words "and died" which A_1 had omitted, or had erroneously translated. But A_2 falls into error by taking "(in)to" as "up to." Also, the "wound" or "blow" inflicted on Ahab, is taken by A_2 as being the "blow," "defeat," or "rout," of the whole army. Hence A_2 apparently describes the blood from the carnage as *rising up* to the bottom of the chariot (compare our "knee-deep in blood," and Rev. xiv. 20, " blood . . . *even unto the bridles of the horses*"), instead of flowing down into it:—

1 K. xxii. 35 : " . . . and died at even, and the blood ran out of the wound into the bottom (lit. hollow) of the chariot," LXX " . . . (A_1) (a_1 ?) *from morning* till evening, and there was poured forth blood from the (b_1) *wound* (c_1) *into* the hollow of the chariot. (A_2) (a_2 ?) *And he died*

---

[1] [98a] Ezra vi. 20 : " As one " ἕως εἷς, probably a Greek error for ὡς εἷς. If the scribe had meant "*to* the last man " would he not have written ἕως ἑνός ? "Because," or "for " (כי), is rendered in Esdr. first ὅτε and then ὅτι.

at even and there went forth the blood (b_2) *of the rout* (c_2) *as far as* the hollow of the chariot."

§ 3. *Hebrew conflations*

[100] It would be scarcely reasonable to suppose that the process of conflation did not influence the Hebrew Scriptures till they began to be translated into Greek. Long before the date of the earliest book of the Septuagint, Hebrew copyists of the Scriptures may well have doubted, for example, between a *d* and an *r*, whether written in Hebrew or Samaritan characters, and may consequently have inserted in the margin a various reading that in due course found its way into the text along with the original reading, as part of a conflation.

[101] Take for example, Ps. xviii. 12 "(a_1) his thick clouds (a_2) passed, (a_3) hail, and coals of fire." The mere fact that these three words are similar in form would hardly lead us to suspect—and certainly would not justify us in believing—that the text was conflated. But the Hebrew word "pass" ($a''br$) is so liable to confusion, and so often confused, that its occurrence must always put us on our guard where there is the least suspicion of error. And we happen to possess another, and, as it is generally believed, earlier version of these words in 2 S. xxii. 13, "*There were kindled* ($ba''r$) coals of fire.*" This at once justifies the suspicion of conflation in the later version, arising from a confusion of $ba''r$ with $a''br$ and other similar words.[1]

[102] In the next instance, a passage in Kings describes the rescue of the child Joash by his aunt Jehosheba, immediately after the death of his father, king Ahaziah. The author calls Jehosheba, "daughter of *king Joram*, and sister of Ahaziah" :—

---

[1] "Were kindled (בערו)," "his thick clouds (עביו)," "passed (עברו)," "hail (ברד)." The word "thick-clouds" occurs in the preceding verse, and the Psalmist may have thought that it was to be repeated here.

2 K. xi. 2: "Jehosheba, *the daughter of king Joram*, sister of Ahaziah, took Joash the son of Ahaziah, and stole him away from among the king's sons that were slain, even him and his nurse [and put them, *or*, who were] in the bedchamber, and they hid him from Athaliah, so that he was not slain."

This is correct. Jehosheba *was* "daughter of *king Joram*," who had preceded his son Ahaziah on the throne. But the author of the parallel passage in Chronicles, perhaps thinking the description of Jehosheba superfluously lengthy, shortens it to "daughter of the king." Now the "king" last mentioned is Ahaziah. This makes the statement inaccurate. At the same time, while condensing the statement of fact into an error, the Chronicler amplifies a harsh and terse construction, "stole him in the bedchamber," softening it into "stole him . . . *and put him* in the bedchamber."[1] This being erroneous as regards Jehosheba's parentage, a corrector added a second and correct version, perhaps written from the priestly point of view, in which he adds that Jehosheba was the wife of Jehoiada the priest. The result is:—

2 Chr. xxii. 11: "(A$_1$) *But*[2] Jehoshabeath, the daughter of *the king*, took Joash the son of Ahaziah, and stole him away from among the king's sons that were slain, *and put him* and his nurse in the bedchamber. (A$_2$) *But*[2] Jehoshabeath, the daughter of king Jehoram, the wife of Jehoiada the priest (for[3] she was the sister of Ahaziah), hid him from Athaliah so that she slew him not."

[1] [102a] Also, the plural agency ("and *they* hid") mentioned in Kings, disappears in Chronicles. The "nurse," in the latter, does not help to hide the child, but *is herself hidden*.

[2] The same Hebrew particle (ו)—which may mean almost any English conjunction—comes at the beginning of all three accounts, 2 K., 2 Chr. (A$_1$), (A$_2$). R.V. has "But" in A$_1$; "So" in A$_2$.

[3] "For" (כי). So R.V., but perhaps "because," or "since," would better express the Hebrew. The writer of A$_2$ suggests by this conjunction that the mention of the relationship is not superfluous. It gives the *reason* for the act that is on the point of being mentioned.

[103] Impassioned language is often abrupt and brief, and leaves much to the imagination. When David was urged to drink the water his warriors had brought him at the hazard of their lives, he exclaimed (2 S. xxiii. 17), (lit.) "Profanation to me, Jehovah, from my doing this! what! The blood of men that went with their lives [in their hands]!" The Revised Version supplies words to make full sense, thus: "*Shall I drink* the blood?" The Authorised Version has, "*Is not this* the blood?" The Hebrew has simply an interrogative prefix, prefixed in the original to "blood," but represented in the translation given above by "what!"

Compare the parallel 1 Chr. xi. 19, "Profanation to me from my God from doing this! The blood of these men (A_1) *shall I drink with their lives?* (A_2) For *with their lives they brought* it." Here, in the first place, Chronicles changes "Jehovah" into "from my God" as being more reverential. Then the writer of A_1 inserts (as our Revised Version does) "shall I drink." But having done this, he is disposed to take "with" along with this insertion in a new sense, " Shall I swallow their blood *together with* their lives?" But (A_2) another view was that "with their lives" must be taken with "they went." Only, if that was to be done, the verb of motion, it seemed, must be taken causatively—"they caused-to-go," or rather, "caused-to-come." Hence the corrector (the writer of A_2) substituted "with their lives *they caused it to come,*" *i.e.* brought it.

§ 4. *Prejudice a cause of error*

[104] Prejudice or bias is an important cause of the corruption of history. But a distinction must be drawn between even the wildest of blunders, when supported by some apparent shadow of evidence, and a mis-statement based on no evidence at all.

Take, as a modern instance, a statement made in a French newspaper, called "La Croix de la Charente," of 4 March 1900, that in English schools there was an atlas of which one map was *France in 1910*, shewing the departments from the Pas de Calais to the Pyrenees as belonging to England.

At the first glance, one might have been ready to assume that no ignorance and no error could account for an assertion so completely at variance with fact and so incompatible with English unimaginative ways and commonplace notions about education; and one might seem driven to the conclusion that it was merely a falsehood, fabricated out of nothing but malignity, and tricked out with details to give it the speciousness of reality.

But it was pointed out, in a letter to the *Times* (28 April 1900), that Green's "Short History of the English People" contains a map of France assigning the above-mentioned provinces to England, but *referring to a remote past, the days of Richard I. Its date is* 1190. This is not very different (in the eyes of a sufficiently prejudiced scribe) from 1910.

§ 5. *The "four sons" of Araunah*

[105] The remarks in the last section bear on the next instance—the last for which space can be found here. It is of special importance because it shews how one initial mistake, perhaps facilitated or favoured by a love of the marvellous, may lead to further mistakes, resulting ultimately in a conversion of a non-miraculous fact into a miracle. And it will be interesting to note that, as usual, the incorrect and miraculous version comes first, while the correct narrative comes last. The original is as follows:—

2 S. xxiv. 19-20—"And David went up according to the saying of Gad as the Lord commanded. And Araunah looked forth and saw *the king and his servants*

passing-over toward him: and Araunah went out and bowed himself before the king with his face to the ground." Now there has been a previous mention of "an angel of the Lord" as being by "the threshing floor of Araunah," and the word "angel" or "messenger" (*mlák*), is easily confused with "king" (*mlk*), and is actually confused with it elsewhere.[1]

[106] The writer of the first clause of the parallel passage in Chronicles actually makes this mistake, and writes "angel" for "king." But, having done this, he is confronted with the difficulty of the angel's "*servants passing-over.*" Now, it happens, that these two words "pass-over" ($a''br$) and "servant" ($a''bd$) differ in nothing but the difference between *r* and *d*. The reader will be prepared (5-7) to believe that they are easily confused together. Moreover, the letters of the phrase "and *his servants passing-over*," resemble those of the phrase, "and *his four sons*."[2]

[107] Again, the Greek for "servants" is also the Greek for "boys," which, in certain contexts, might mean "sons."[3] If therefore the Hebrew of Chronicles was written after Samuel had been translated into Greek, and if the

---

[1] [105a] "King (מלך)." "messenger (מלאך)." The Hebrew "messenger" is rendered by the Greek "king" or "ruler," in Is. xiv. 32, xlii. 19; Prov. xiii. 17. On the confusion of "king" and "messenger," or "angel," see Dr. Ginsburg's *Introduction to the Hebrew Bible*, 141: "In 2 K. vii. 17, we have the primitive form המלך = הַמֶּלֶךְ = הַמַּלְאָךְ 'the messenger' without *Aleph*, as is attested by the Septuagint and the Syriac. The passage ought accordingly to be translated 'when the *messenger* came down to him.' This is corroborated by the statement in the preceding chapter, viz. vi. 33. Exactly the reverse is the case in 2 S. xi. 1, where the Massorah itself tells us that the redactors of the text inserted *Aleph* into this very word, converting (הַמְּלָבִים) 'kings' into (הַמַּלְאָכִים) '*messengers.*'"

[2] The former = ואתעבדיועברים, the latter = וארבעתבנים.

[3] [107a] Comp. Acts iii. 13 παῖς, (R.V.) txt. "Servant" (marg. "'Child': and so in ver. 26; iv. 27, 30"). The centurion's servant healed by Jesus is called in Matt. viii. 8 παῖς, (R.V.) "servant" (marg. "boy"), but in Luke vii. 2 δοῦλος, "servant." A similar narrative in Jn. iv. 46f., describes the healing of a nobleman's "son" (υἱός), called also in the context παιδίον and παῖς.

Greek version of Samuel contained this ambiguous word, the Jewish writer or reviser of Chronicles might be led by a tradition derived from the Greek translation of Samuel to suppose that a fuller version of the story contained some mention of "boys," that is to say, Araunah's "sons." The Chronicler's acceptance of this reading would be facilitated also by the unusual nature of the verb " passing-over " applied to David's retinue.[1]

[108] But when Araunah's "four sons" were thus introduced into the story, it became needful to adjust the context to the new insertion. "His four sons *toward him*" would make no sense; it must be "his four sons *with him*." This involved no very great change.[2] But it was naturally asked how the "sons" came to be there, and what part (if any) they played in this solemn, inaugural act—a kind of anticipation of the building of the Temple—where they might well seem out of place. These questions were perhaps originally answered in the margin. The "four sons" played no part at all, except that of suggesting reverence to future readers. They "hid themselves." And the reason for their presence was that they were helping their father in his work, "now Ornan was threshing wheat." Thus the foundations are laid for an entirely new version of the story.

[109] It only remained to transfer these graphic touches from the margin to the text, and to modify a few of the expressions in Samuel that did not seem exact, or did not quite harmonise with the additions made in Chronicles. For example, it was not strictly true to say that "*the Lord* commanded." It was more exact to describe the message as "the saying of Gad which he spake in the name of the Lord." Again, in the Bible, when people see an angel, they

---

[1] Our R.V. alters it to "coming on"; but that does not express the Hebrew meaning which the R.V. gives in the margin.
[2] "Toward him (עליו)," "with him (עמו)."

do not usually "look forth" as from a window and behold it. More frequently they unexpectedly see an angel behind them, or by their side. So Araunah "turns back and sees" it. We are now prepared for the new version, or rather for the first clause of it, introducing the "four sons":—

(A_1) 1 Chr. xxi. 19-20 : "And David went up at the saying of Gad, which he spake in the name of the Lord. And Ornan turned back and saw *the angel.* And his four sons [that were] with him hid themselves.[1] Now Ornan was threshing wheat."

[110] In the next sentence, the corrector gives the right tradition without any miraculous adjuncts, dropping the "servants" or "sons" altogether, and filling up the space by clauses that add definiteness. Instead of "went up," he has "came to Ornan." Instead of "looked forth," he has "looked intently and saw David"; and, after "went out," he adds, "of the threshing floor."[2] The result is—

(A_2) 1 Chr. xxi. 21 : "And as David came to Ornan, Ornan looked intently and saw David and went out of the threshing floor and bowed himself to David with his face to the ground."

No one of course will deny that the original narrative in Samuel recognizes an angel as God's agent producing a pestilence : and, so far, the original may be called "miraculous." But that is very different from the miraculousness implied in the story as developed by the Chronicler.

[111] The existence of conflations in Hebrew shows (what ought indeed to need no showing) that *they do not necessarily prove translation.* They prove simply this, the

---

[1] 1 Chr. xxi. 20: "hid themselves (מתחבאים)." The LXX, in perplexity, transliterates this, καὶ τέσσαρας υἱοὺς αὐτοῦ μετ' αὐτοῦ μεθαχαβείν.

[2] [110a] Such defining additions form a large part of the details of the edition of Mark used by Matthew and Luke. See 534. "Looked intently" is the literal meaning of the Hebrew.

existence of an original that seemed to a copyist or translator to be obscure, or inadequate, or both. They would therefore naturally arise in the copying of a difficult book (like Job or Thucydides) or of a work become, or becoming, antiquated (like Chaucer). Chronicles is supposed to have been written after the exile, at a time when the old Hebrew (now called Samaritan) characters of the Bible were being exchanged for the existing square characters, and when the language of the pre-exilic period had become archaic and almost foreign. If so, it was of the nature of a semi-translation.

[112] The one condition needed for the growth of conflations (in addition to supposed obscurity or inadequacy) is that the text should not be as yet fixed by general acceptance. And, of course, as long as a written tradition is not only recent but also environed by pre-existing oral traditions, it is in a state of non-authoritativeness that renders it peculiarly liable to be conflated. The phenomena of Chronicles support, instead of shaking, the conclusion that a conflated Gospel, like that of Mark, is probably earlier than comparatively non-conflated Gospels like those of Matthew and Luke. This will be shown more clearly in the next chapter.

CHAPTER VI

CONFLATIVE VERSIONS

§ 1. *The First Book of Esdras*

[113] Several parallel passages have been given above from the Greek translations of Esdras and Ezra, in which it has been shown that the former contains conflations where the latter does not. And the mistakes in the former are so numerous as compared with those in the latter that it is reasonable to suppose that the latter is the more recent of the two translations. But there are passages where the Greek of Esdras is closer to the Hebrew than that of Ezra. For example, where the Greek of Ezra has "I rent my garments and *quaked-for-fear*," Esdras has correctly, though freely, "I rent my garments and *the-holy-raiment*," the Hebrew being "my *mantle*."[1] The following passages afford a useful warning that sometimes a loose and inaccurate version may in some single point lead us back to the original Hebrew where the closer Hebraic rendering fails to do so :—

[114] Ezra ix. 1 : (Hebr.) (lit.) " There have not been separated the people of Israel and the priests and the Levites from the peoples of the lands, [but have done] like-

---

[1] Ezra ix. 3, 5 (1 Esdr. viii. 68, 70): מעילי, ἐπαλλόμην. The מעיל was a mantle worn by women and the upper classes but also by priests. Tromm. suggests that the LXX read עליה; but does this ever mean "shake"? More probably the LXX read מעד which means "totter," and is rendered σαλεύω in 2 S. xxii. 37, and ἀσθενεῖν in the parallel Ps. xviii. 36.

[115] CONFLATIVE VERSIONS

their-abominations, those-of (lit. to) the Canaanite, the Hittite, the Perizzite, the Jebusite, the Ammonite, the Moabite, the *Mitzrite* (*i.e.* Egyptian), and the Amorite."
1 Esdr. viii. 66 (R.V. 65): "There *have not* separated both the rulers, and the priests, and the Levites, *and* foreign nations of the land, their uncleannesses, [those] of Canaanaeans and Chettaeans and Pherezaeans, and Jebusaeans, and Moabites, and *Egyptians* and *Idumaeans*." [1]

The Greek of Ezra is perhaps influenced by a reaction from the loose inaccuracy of Esdras. It follows the Hebrew exactly except that it probably alters the particle "like" to the very similar "in," [2] concluding thus: "to-the (dat.) Canaanei, the (nom.) Hethei, [3] the Pheresthei, the Jebusei, the Ammonei, the Moab, the *Moserei*, and the Amorei." If this were found in a Gospel where no Hebrew original is extant, we should be perplexed by "Moserei," till we found a parallel "Egyptian" in another Gospel. Then we should infer that both represented a Hebrew original "Mitzree" or "Mitzrite," the regular name for "Egyptian."

Thus, in the above passage, though teeming with inaccuracies, Esdras has preserved a clue to the Hebrew obscured in the Greek Ezra.

[115] In the next, Esdras has probably preserved the true Hebrew, where it has been corrupted in our present text, in which it runs thus (2 Chr. xxxv. 21): "I came not against thee this day, but against the house wherewith I have

---

[1] (i.) "People of Israel" = עם ישראל. The translator could hardly corrupt this into anything meaning rulers. More probably he considered that the original was loose, because "people" included priests and Levites. (ii.) The letter (מ), signifying "from" ("*from* the peoples"), happening to follow the same letter at the end of "Levites," is dropped, to the ruin of the sense. (iii.) The letter signifying "like" (כ) is omitted without any excuse. (iv.) Also אמר ("Amorite") is taken as אדם ("Idumaean") (6).

[2] [114a] "Like (כ)," and " in (ב)," are repeatedly confused; and the latter might be taken to mean "in the way of," "according to."

[3] Τῷ Χαναvεί, ὁ 'Εθεί, ὁ . . . The change of case probably represents an attempt to show that the Hebrew "to" occurs only before the first name.

68

war." The literal Hebrew is "the-house-of-my-war." But although "house" is freely used for "place of," "receptacle of," it would be difficult to find a use like this. By a slight corruption, "house-of" might spring from "Euphrates," which is the reading of 1 Esdr. i. 25 (R.V. 27): "for on the Euphrates is my war."[1]

[116] In view of a passage in the Synoptic Gospels where Matthew and Luke agree in describing Jesus as "passing the night," while Mark only speaks of Him as "going," it will be useful to note Ezra x. 6 : "(a) *And* [Ezra] *went* into the chamber . . . (b) *and he went* thither ; bread he ate not." This makes no sense. Yet, as the Hebrew for "he went" is precisely the same in (a) and (b) it seems unjustifiable to give different translations (*e.g.*) "(b) and [when] he *came*." But the Greek of the parallel 1 Esdr. ix. 2 reads "*and he-passed-the-night* there," a phrase very easily confused with "and he went."[2]

[117] In its general character, Esdras, as compared with Ezra, is not only a free translation, but also grossly inaccurate on points of history and chronology. No one would blame such substitutions as "temple" for "house of God," and "Coele-Syria" for "beyond Jordan," and "the God that created heaven" for "the God of heaven." Mere adaptations like these are quite compatible with regard for historic truth.[3]

---

[1] "House-of"=בית; "Euphrates"=פרת. "But" and "for" are equally justifiable as renderings of כי; אל="to," "against," "near." The Greek of Esdras makes better sense. The Greek of Chr. has πόλεμον πολεμῆσαι, instead of "but against the house of my war."

In the preceding verse, 2 Chr. xxxv. 20, "against *Carchemish* by Euphrates," the LXX of Chr. omits "Carchemish," while that of Esdras inserts it. Esdras is, perhaps, more accurate when parallel to Chronicles than when parallel to Ezra.

[2] [116a] "And he went (וילך)," "and he passed the night (וילן)." See Mk. xi. 19, 20, "They went forth outside the city. And passing along . . . "; Mt. xxi. 17, "He went forth outside the city to Bethany and *passed the night* there"; Lk. xxi. 37, "Coming forth he *passed the night* on the mountain" (**450**).

[3] Some of these substitutions remind us of Luke, who never uses "sea"

But the author hopelessly confuses the leading facts of the return from exile by reading history backwards, placing Artaxerxes before Darius, and Darius before Cyrus. He also introduces the famous apocryphal discussion as to "What is greatest?" giving the leading part in it to Zerubbabel and making it the immediate cause of the rebuilding of the Temple.

§ 2. *The Septuagint Version of Daniel*

[118] Such, then, is the character of one of the two most conflative books of the Septuagint. The other—its rival in the insertion of apocryphal matter as well as in conflations—is the Septuagint version of the book of Daniel.[1] In comparing this with the far more accurate version by Theodotion, we have the great advantage of knowing that Theodotion lived in the second century of the Christian era, long after the date of the Septuagint translation. That he knew and used the latter is proved by his close conformity with it in many passages, and indeed in almost all where it accurately represents the Hebrew. In others, the relation between the two will be discerned from the following passages:—

[119] Dan. ii. 8 : "The thing (lit. word) is gone from me." This may mean ("word" being regularly used for "matter" or "business" in Hebrew) "The *matter* [*i.e.* the nature of my dream] has *vanished* from my memory"; and Theodotion takes it so.[2] But R.V. margin gives an alterna-

(always "lake") to describe the sea of Gennesaret or Tiberias. Luke also never uses the phrase "beyond Jordan."

[1] In quoting from this book, which is of a composite character, the word Hebrew may sometimes be loosely used for Aramaic.

[2] [119*a*] Dan. ii. 8 : Theod. ἀπέστη ἀπ' ἐμοῦ τὸ ῥῆμα. Following the Hebrew, he uses "word" where we should say "matter"; so in Kings and Chronicles "the *acts*" of a king are regularly called in Hebrew "the words," and rendered sometimes ῥήματα, sometimes πράγματα. Ἀπέστη, *i.e.* "departed," clearly shows that the meaning is not "was issued." In that case, ἐξῆλθεν would have been employed.

tive. "The word is gone forth from me that . . ." *i.e.* "I have irrevocably decreed that . . ." In Dan. ii. 5, where the phrase occurs for the first time, the LXX took it as Theodotion takes it here; but in the present passage the LXX conflates thus : "(A_1) the business is gone from me; (A_2) as therefore I have ordained so shall it be."[1]

[120] Dan. xii. 8 : "What shall be the *issue* (marg. *latter end*) of these things?" Two interpretations are possible. The first is literal, referring merely to time—"What shall be the consequence, or final results, of these things?" So Theodotion, "What [shall be] the last of these things?"[2] The second regards the "final outcome" as a conclusion, symmetrically completing, and hence indirectly *explaining*, the mysterious events that had preceded. Adopting this latter interpretation the LXX tries to express it in two free paraphrases :—"(A_1) What [is] the *solution* of this word? (A_2) and to whom [or what] [belong] these *dark-sayings*?"[3]

[121] Dan. xi. 31 : "and *arms* shall stand on his part"; the Hebrew noun, in the singular, may mean "arm" (not in the military sense, but the bodily "arm") regarded as symbolizing strength. But it may also mean "seed," "offspring." Theodotion takes the word as meaning "offspring"; but in this sense, the word is not used in the plural. The LXX has "arms." This, then, is one of the very few cases where the LXX is more accurate than Theodotion. Some MSS. of Theodotion conflate "arms" and "offspring."[4]

*[122] Dan. iv. 29 (Aram. 26) "[The king] was walking in (marg. "upon") the royal palace of Babylon," lit. "On his

---

[1] Dan. ii. 8 : LXX, (A_1) ἀπέστη ἀπ' ἐμοῦ τὸ πρᾶγμα. As A_1 was the form used above (Dan. ii. 5), it seems probable that A_2 occurred on second thoughts to a scribe or editor at this point. At first it may have seemed to deserve a place in the margin. Then it was placed second in the text.

[2] Τί τὰ ἔσχατα τούτων;

[3] Τίς ἡ λύσις τοῦ λόγου τούτου, καὶ τίνος αἱ παραβολαὶ αὗται;

[4] Dan. xi. 31 : "Arms (זרעים))" LXX, βραχίονες, Theod. σπέρματα, AQ (in Theod.) βραχίονες καὶ σπέρματα.

palace *of the kingdom* that [belongs to] Babylon walking he was." The word here translated "palace" is generally applied to "the palace of the Eternal," that is, to the Temple. But here "palace of the kingdom," or "palace of royalty," means "the royal palace." The LXX takes it in a first paraphrase (A_1) as meaning "walls." Also the LXX seems to convert "Babylon" into "the city" and implies "royal" in the notion of walking "in state." Then it adds (A_2) a briefer translation in which "palace" is rendered "towers." The result is: "The king (A_1) on the *walls* of the city in all his glory was walking about, and (A_2) on its *towers* he was passing."[1]

Theodotion has the following literal rendering: "on the *temple* of his kingdom in Babylon walking about."

[123] Dan. iv. 31 (Aram. 28): "Yet [was the] word in the mouth of the king," *i.e.* "the king had scarcely spoken." "Word" in Aramaic closely resembles "fulfil" in Hebrew. "Yet" is easily corrupted into "upon." The LXX renders "word" first (A_1) correctly, and then (A_2) paraphrases the clause incorrectly, thus: "(A_1) The (a_1) *word* being (b_1) *still* in the mouth of the king (A_2) and (b_2) *upon* the (a_2) *fulfilment* of his word." Theod. "The word being still in the mouth of the king."[2]

*[124] Dan. vi. 17 (Aram.): (lit.) "that there might not

---

[1] Dan. iv. 29 "palace (היכל)"=(Tromm.) βάρις (1), βασίλειον (1), ναός (51), οἶκος (16), ὀχύρωμα (1): (Aram.) ναός (7), οἶκος (5). Here it is rendered by LXX, (A_1) τειχῶν (A_2) πύργων, Theod. ναῷ. "Walking about"=περιεπάτει, "passing" =διεπορεύετο. Possibly LXX may have read כבד δόξα for בבל "Babylon"; but it is not likely that it should have corrupted so common a name.

[2] [123*a*] "Word"=מלתא, "fulfill"=מלא. "Still"=עוד=ἔτι. "Upon"=על =ἐπί. Comp. Mark ix. 6 "he knew not what to answer," with the parallels Matt. xvii. 5, "while he was still speaking," Luke ix. 34, "while he was saying these things." There the original was probably "still was the word *to him* in his mouth." Mark interpreted לו, *i.e.* "to him," as לא, *i.e.* "not," a frequent confusion, as in 2 K. viii. 10 (R.V. txt. and marg.), 2 S. xvi. 18 "his" but Heb. txt. "not," etc. Hence the rendering "he no longer had a word to say." Also he may have confused עוד "yet" with ידע "know." See 422.

be changed *matter* in Daniel," *i.e.* "that nothing might be changed concerning Daniel." Theodotion translates literally, as above. But the Aramaic word "matter" occurs only here, and R.V. gives the marginal alternative "purpose." The LXX, very probably not knowing what the word meant and guessing at the sense, gives a double paraphrase "(A_1) that Daniel might not be delivered from them (*i.e.* from his enemies) (A_2) or that the king might not draw him up out of the den." In A_2, the use of "him" for "Daniel" indicates that A_2 was written after A_1.

*[125] The following is an instance of conflation (owing to Aramaic corruption), combined with Hellenistic paraphrase and a kind of "plunging at the sense."

The literal Aramaic is Dan. v. 30-31 : "In that night was slain Belshazzar, king of the Chaldeans, and Darius the Mede received the kingdom being like-a-son of sixty-two years." The Septuagint, in the first clause of its conflation, translates "in that" as "came," and "night" as "consummation" or "final judgment."[1] In the second, it translates, as elsewhere, "slain" by "utterly taken away,"[2] "king" as kingdom (dropping "Belshazzar" and "in that night."[3]) Then, having inserted a clause to say that "the kingdom

---

[1] "In that"=בה, "came" (ἐπῆλθε)=בא. "By night"=בליליא (Aramaic), "consummation" (σύγκριμα)=בליון (Is. x. 22).

[2] [125a] There are curious facts about the LXX rendering of קטל "slay," which suggest that LXX may have been misled by its correspondence to the Greek ἀναιρεῖν which may mean, in the active, "slay," but, in the middle, "take away." Theod. uses ἀναιρεῖν (4)=קטל "slay," LXX never. In Dan. ii. 14, where Theod. has ἀναιρεῖν, LXX has ἐξάγειν "lead forth [? to execution]." In Dan. v. 19 (Theod.) ἀνῄρει, LXX omits the whole context. In A_2 here Theod. has ἀνῃρέθη, "was slain," LXX=ἐξῆρται, "hath been taken away" (with a possible meaning "destroyed"). In Dan. vii. 11, "I beheld even till the beast *was slain* (Theod. ἀνῃρέθη) and his body destroyed, and he was given to be burned with fire," the LXX has ἀπετυμπανίσθη καὶ ἀπώλετο τὸ σῶμα αὐτοῦ (L. and S.) "cudgelled to death," but more probably "tortured to death" as in 3 Mac. iii. 27).

[3] Possibly, in A_2, the LXX took "consummation," *i.e.* making an utter end, as "utterly": and considered it implied in the ἐξ in ἐξῆρται "*utterly* taken away."

was given to the Medes and Persians," it substitutes for "Darius," "Artaxerxes the of the Medes." This *ought* to mean "the man of that name belonging to the Medes"; but perhaps "Artaxerxes" is used as the Persian title for king, and the LXX means "the Artaxerxes (*i.e.* king) of the Medes."[1] In the next verse the LXX mentions "Darius" as old and renowned, but drops the number of his years.[2] The result is: "(A_1) And (a_1) the final judgment (b_1) came upon Baltasar the (c_1) king (A_2) and (c_2) the kingdom (?a_2) *was utterly taken away* (b_2 om.) from the Chaldeans, and was given to the Medes and the Persians, and Artaxerxes, he of the Medes [or, the Artaxerxes, *i.e.* king of the Medes], received the kingdom. And Darius [was] full of days and renowned in old age."

§ 3. *Conflations arising from Aramaic*

[126] It was natural that Greek translators, familiar with Hebrew rather as a written than as a spoken language, should sometimes take an Aramaic word in its Hebrew signification. Or they might use a MS. in which the Aramaic equivalent of difficult Hebrew words was frequently written in the margin. This might lead to an abundance of conflations.

[127] For example, take Dan. iv. 19 : "Then Daniel, whose name [was] Belteshazzar, was astonied for *a while* (lit. for *one glance*, A.V. *one hour*), and his thoughts troubled him." In a preceding passage the meaning of the word here translated (A.V.) "hour" appears to correspond to our "at that *instant*,"[3] but it is there translated in both versions by

[1] Dan. v. 31 (LXX), Ἀρταξέρξης ὁ τῶν Μήδων.

[2] [125*b*] This is because the LXX stumbles at the Aramaic idiom "a son of sixty-two years" for "sixty-two years old." It takes כבר "like a son" as כבר "renowned" (the frequent error (5-7) of interchanging *r* and *d*).

[3] [127*a*] Dan. iii. 6 : "Whoso falleth not down . . . shall the same *instant* (but R.V. *hour*) be cast into the . . . furnace." Comp. Taylor's *Jewish Fathers*, iv. 24.

the Greek "hour," which often means "season," "appointed time," etc. In Hebrew, however, the word exists only as a verb, meaning "look (for help)," "look (in dismay)," etc. It is also liable to be confused with words meaning "shudder," and "to be altered [in countenance]." Theodotion follows the Aramaic. But the Septuagint appears to have at first taken it as meaning "perplexity," so that it intensified the "wonder" and might be rendered "greatly." Then it seems to have accumulated a number of phrases expressive of intense wonder, and finally to have given the correct, or, at all events, the literal rendering, with this result:—"But (a_1) *greatly* did Daniel wonder, and thoughts made him afraid (lit. hastened him); and (? a_3) having feared, (? a_4) trembling having possessed him, and (? a_5) his aspect being altered, having shaken his head, having wondered (a_2) *one hour.*" It is probable that some of these clumsy participial phrases placed one after the other without connecting particles, are attempts at rendering "whose name was Belteshazzar." But facts indicate that two of them (besides (a_1)) are conflations of "hour."[1]

[1] [127*b*] "Hour (שעה)" might be confused with שער "shudder," and possibly (though less easily) with שנא "alter."

BOOK II
THE SYNOPTIC GOSPELS

CHAPTER I

SPECIMENS OF CONFLATION [1]

THE discussion of all the probable Synoptic conflations must be reserved for a complete Synoptic commentary. A few instances, however, will be given here to shew the application of the rules deduced from the Septuagint.

§ 1. (*Mark*) "*The surrounding country of Galilee*"

Mark i. 28

"And there went forth the report of him everywhere into all the (a_1) *surrounding country* (a_2) *of Galilee*."

Luke iv. 37

"And there proceeded forth a loud rumour about him into every place of the (a_1) *surrounding country*."

[128] "Galilee" means "circuit," and hence "surrounding-country." In the Old Testament, "Galilee" and "region" or "district" are found as alternatives. Maccabees speaks of "all *Galilee* of the Philistines," meaning "all the *region* of the Philistines."[2] Mark conflates the two meanings.

---

[1] The chapter on Septuagint confusions preceded that on Septuagint conflations. Consistently, therefore, the chapter on Synoptic confusions ought to precede that on Synoptic conflations. But the appreciation of the error of conflation—applying, as it often does, not to mere pairs of words, but to long statements of fact and to narratives practically rewritten—is of so much more importance, that it has been thought best to place a few specimens of Synoptic conflation immediately after those of conflation in the Septuagint.

It is assumed throughout this chapter that Mark contains the Triple Tradition from which Matthew and Luke borrowed. See below (**321**).

[2] 1 Mac. v. 15, comp. Joel iii. (iv.) 4: "All the *regions* (גלילות) of Philistia,"

SYNOPTIC CONFLATIONS

But compare :—

Mark i. 14	Matt. iv. 12, 17	Luke iv. 14
"There came Jesus into (a_1) *Galilee* (b_1) *preaching* the Gospel of God."	"He retired into (a_1) *Galilee*.... From that time began Jesus (b_1) *to-preach*."	"(A_1) Jesus turned back . . . into (a_1) *Galilee*, and (A_2) (b_2) *a fame* went forth in the whole of (a_2) *the surrounding country* about him."

[129] Here we must bear in mind that the Greek word (in Mark i. 28) translated "report" may mean not only the report *about* a person, but also the report brought *by* him, as when Isaiah says: "Lord, who hath believed our *report?*" *i.e.*, as usually taken, our *message*, or *preaching*.[1]

Luke appears to have conflated "Galilee" as (a_1) "Galilee," (a_2) "surrounding country," and to have taken (b_1) "preaching" as (b_2) "fame." Thence arises a new tradition (A_2) out of (a_2) and (b_2).

§ 2. (Mark lit.), "*It having become late, when the sun had set*"

Mark i. 32 (lit.)[2]	Matth. viii. 16 (lit.)[2]	Luke iv. 40 (lit.)[2]
"But (a_1) it having become late, (a_2) when the sun had set."	"But (a_1) it having become late."	"But (a_2) the sun setting."

[130] Mark's Greek word "late" occurs only once in the whole of the Septuagint, and then only in Judith. The word and the participial form of the phrase are characteristic

πᾶσα Γαλιλαία ἀλλοφύλων. In Is. ix. 1, "*Galilee* (גליל) of the nations," R.V. has marg. "*district.*" Comp. Josh. xxii. 11: the *region-about* (A.V. "borders-of") Jordan," Γαλααδ (Α Γαλιλωθ) τοῦ Ἰορδ. ; Ezek. xlvii. 8: "the *region* towards the east," τὴν Γαλιλαίαν τὴν πρὸς ἀνατολάς.

[1] Is. liii. 1 (LXX) τῇ ἀκοῇ ἡμῶν, quoted thus in Jn. xii. 38, Rom. x. 16.

[2] Here, as in several other translated passages in this book, the English is sacrificed to the object of expressing, or approximating to, the idiom of the original.

of idiomatic Greek. Probably a_1 represents the first free translation of the original, conflated with a_2, a subsequent literal translation. Matthew prefers a_1, Luke a_2 (only in the participial form).[1]

§ 3 (Mark lit.), "*It* (*i.e. the seed*) *arose* . . . *there arose the sun.*"

Mark iv. 5, 6 (lit.)	Matth. xiii. 5 (lit.)	Luke viii. 6 (lit.)
"And other fell on the rocky [land] where it had not much earth, and straightway it arose because it had no depth of earth; and when there arose the sun it was burned up, and because it had no root it withered."	"But others fell on the rocky [lands] where they had not much earth; and straightway they arose because they had no depth of earth, and, the sun rising, they were burned up, and because they had no root they withered."	"And other fell down on the rock, and having grown, it withered, because it had no moisture."

[131] Here we have to do, not with the words of an evangelist, but with those of Jesus. And it is highly improbable that Luke would have omitted the clause relating to the sun if he had believed Jesus to have uttered it. We are driven to conclude either that (i.) Luke's original did not contain the words, or that, although it contained them, (ii.) they appeared to Luke to be based on some error.

(i.) The English of Mark, above, follows Mark's Greek order. But by transposition, the Greek might run in the order of the following sentence, in which a bracket encloses the words intervening between the end of the first "arose" and the end of the second :—

---

[1] [130*a*] Luke wishes to say, not (as Mk.) "when the sun *had* set," but "when the sun *was setting*." But the Greek verb (δῦναι) has no imperfect indicative in common use. Luke resorts to the present participle.

"It *arose* [because it had no depth of earth, and it was burned up when the sun *arose*], and because it had no root it withered away." In this shape, the sentence is liable to the error called "homoioteleuton."[1] Now it is probable (**325a**) that our present text of Mark has come to us through several editions ; and if one of these, containing the Greek in this order, was employed by Luke (or by some author followed by Luke), his eye may have passed from "arose" to "arose," causing him to omit the intervening words. This is possible, but on the whole not likely, for the following reasons :—

[**132**] (ii.) Where Mark has "root," Luke has a very rare word indeed, meaning "moisture," "juice," "sap," etc. Now this is difficult to explain on the hypothesis that Luke was merely following a corrupt text of Mark ; for the general tendency of corruption is to substitute an easy word for a difficult and a familiar word for a rare one, and not *vice versa*. But it is easy to explain on the hypothesis that Luke thought he was restoring the exact meaning of an original Hebrew text.[2] Luke's Greek word may mean "moisture in the earth," but it may mean "internal moisture," "sap," "vitality." Now, if the Hebrew word was of a rare and technical kind, the passage might fall under the head of conflations from technical terms, described above (**69**). A Hebrew word meaning "freshness," "greenness," or "moisture," causing the earliest translators to doubt whether it referred to the plant or to the root, might lead them to

---

[1] [**131a**] That is, the error of passing in transcription from the termination of one passage (*e.g.*, "*arose*") to the *similar* termination of a second consecutive passage (*e.g.*, "*arose*"), omitting the second termination and all the words that precede it up to the first termination (*e.g.*, "because it had . . . the sun *arose*"). Homoioteleuton means "similar termination."

[2] Lk. viii. 13 agrees with Mk. iv. 17 in having "root" when the context speaks no longer about seeds but about souls. Supposing Luke's "moisture" to have been the original, Mk. iv. 6 may have been influenced by Mk. iv. 17. The translator or editor of Mk. iv. 6, casting about for some rendering of an obscure Hebrew word in the earlier passage, bethought himself that in the corresponding part of the explanation later on, mention was made of "root."

paraphrase it as "depth of earth," "much earth," "root," etc."[1] To this must be added that the Greek word "(a)rise," though applied in the Septuagint to plants as well as to the sun, is more frequently applied to the latter; and indeed the noun "rising" is regularly used for the "sun-rise" or "east."

[133] That Mark has gone wrong through conflation seems, on the whole, more probable than that Luke has gone wrong through homoioteleuton. This probability will be greatly strengthened if it is shown hereafter that Mark is habitually conflative. For the present, as a working hypothesis, we take this as the Hebrew original: "And other fell on the rock and it (a)rose (*i.e.*, grew up), and because it had no moisture it withered." At a very early period, "rock," seeming hyperbolical—for what could grow on a rock?— was changed to "rocky land(s)"; "(a)rose" was explained in the margin by the suggestion of "the sun"; "moisture" was explained as being "depth of earth," or "much earth," or "root." Hence arose various traditions: "(A_1) it grew up because it had no depth of earth, and withered away;" "(A_2) because it had no root it withered away"; "(A_3) the sun rose and it was burned up." All these Mark conflated. Matthew followed him. Luke not only omitted the additions but also substituted for the ambiguous word "(a)rose," the word "grew up," and also returned to the literal though difficult "rock."[2]

§ 4. (*Mark*) "*Why are ye fearful? Have ye not yet faith?*"

Mark iv. 40	Matth. viii. 26	Luke viii. 25
(a_1) "Why are ye fearful? (a_2) Have ye not yet faith?"	(a_1) "Why are ye fearful, (a_2) O ye of little faith?"	(a_2) "Where is your faith?"

[1] The rare word אך, translated by LXX "root" in Job viii. 12, means "freshness," "greenness." In its Talm. form, אוך, "hollow," it might possibly be confused with the hollow, or depth, of the earth, being once rendered ἐκ τῆς γῆς φωνεῖν.

[2] "Rocky"=Mk. τὸ πετρῶδες, Mt. τὰ πετρώδη: "(a)rose"=(ἐξ)ανέτειλεν.

[134] The Greek word here rendered "fearful" occurs only thrice as the representation of a Hebrew word in the Septuagint; but a_1 would be a very natural way of expressing in vernacular Greek some Hebrew idiom reproaching the disciples for want of steadfastness. There is therefore an antecedent probability that Luke omitted a_1 as being a paraphrase of the more literal a_2.

[135] As regards a_2, the differences point to some Hebrew particle that might mean "Where?" implying the answer "Nowhere." Matthew's compound ("little-faithed") is essentially Greek. "Little,"—thus used as part of a compound adjective — is very rare in the Septuagint:[1] but "little-faithed" is used four times by Matthew and is once adopted by Luke.[2] It might represent the Hebrew "dull (lit. heavy) of heart." But here Mark and Luke point to an original "no-faith" or "where-faith?"

[136] The latter view is confirmed by the Hebrew use of "where" to signify negation, as in the name "Ichabod," which means literally "*where* [*is*] glory," but implies "the glory *is departed* from Israel."[3] Compare also the Hebrew, "man giveth up the ghost *and where is he?*" with the Greek, "but a mortal, having fallen, exists *no more*."[4] Mark appears to have taken this particle negatively, with an implied interrogative, "Ye have *not yet* faith [it seems]," Luke interrogatively, while Matthew expressed it by a paraphrase.[5]

---

[1] Only in ὀλιγόψυχος (6), and ὀλιγόβιος (2).

[2] "Little-faithed (ὀλιγόπιστοι)," Mt. vi. 30 (Lk. xii. 28), viii. 26, xiv. 31, xvi. 8.

[3] 1 S. iv. 21 R.V. marg. "there-is-no (אי) glory," LXX οὐαὶ-βαρ-χαβώθ, apparently taking אי in its meaning "woe," "woe,-son-of-glory."

[4] Job xiv. 10, πεσὼν δὲ βροτὸς οὐκέτι ἐστίν.

[5] [136a] The exact words of the original must remain doubtful. Mark's text is itself not quite certain. W. and H. read οὔπω, but Tisch. οὔτως; πῶς οὐκ. (a) אי = "where" or "not," (b) איך = "how," (c) איכה = "where" or "how," (d) כה = "thus." We should expect (b) when prefixed to (d) to mean πῶς οὔτως, but in Cant. v. 3 it means "how."

§ 5. (*Luke*) lit. "*Fearing they wondered.*" *Conflated?*

Mark iv. 41	Matth. viii. 27	Luke viii. 25
"And they feared a great fear and began to say to one another, Who then is this that even the wind and the sea obey him?"	"But the men wondered saying, What kind [of man] is this that even the winds and the sea obey him?"	"But fearing they wondered saying to one another, Who then is this that even the winds he commandeth and the water and they obey him?"

(i) (Luke) "*fearing they wondered.*"

[**137**] Are we to regard this as a conflate? Not exactly. The original was probably the reduplicated verb and verbal, or verb and noun, "fearing they feared," or "they feared a fear." Mark—who often elsewhere alone preserves the Hebrew reduplication [1]—preserves the Hebrew here, but adds "great" for emphasis. The Septuagint frequently ignores the Hebrew reduplication, and so does Matthew here. His Greek word for "what-kind-of" shows that he is not following a Hebraic style.[2] Luke avoids the literal reduplication, but expresses it by two verbs.

[**136*b***] Mk. vii. 18 (Mt. xv. 16) οὕτως (Mt. ἀκμὴν) καὶ ὑμεῖς ἀσύνετοί ἐστε, suggests that Mt. read עד כה "up to this extent," where Mk. read כה.

[**136*c***] Mk. viii. 17-18 has, instead of the parall. (Mt. xvi. 8) "[why reason ye] in *yourselves, O ye of little faith?*" a lengthy equivalent "(nor) do ye understand? have ye your heart hardened [or, blinded]? Having eyes see ye not, and having ears hear ye not?" It is most improbable that Mt. would have omitted all this if he had believed that it was rightly assigned to Jesus. But compare Jer. v. 21, "O foolish people *and without understanding* (lit. *and there is no heart*), who have eyes and see not, who have ears and hear not." It is possible that the original contained Jeremiah's phrase "and there is no heart," and that an early evangelist added to Mark Jeremiah's context—in order to explain the force of the prophet's phrase.

[1] [**137*a***] For instances of reduplication of cognate noun and verb in Mk. alone, see Mk. i. 26, iii. 28, v. 42, xv. 34 (comp. xiii. 19, 20). Lk. xxiii. 46 (compared with Mk. xv. 37) is an exception.

[2] Mt. viii. 27, "What kind of (ποταπός)" occurs (in the LXX) only in Dan. (LXX) Su. 54.

[138] Luke's use of two different verbs does not arise from mere love of variety. A Hebrew verbal derived from the Hebrew "fear" regularly means "wonder," and Luke may have felt that to a Greek ear the meaning of "awe" was better conveyed by combining "fear" and "wonder," than by "fear" alone.[1]

[139] Matthew's "men" probably arose from his misunderstanding the Hebrew idiom for "(they spoke) *to one another*," which (it will be observed) he omits. It is "(they spoke) *man to neighbour* (or, *to brother*)." Hence Ezra uses "man" where Esdras uses "each," and a Greek sentence such as "*a man* took" may represent a Hebrew original *each man* took."[2] The original may have been "Fearing they feared and said man to neighbour." Matthew rendered this freely, "the men wondered and said."

(ii.) (Luke) "*he commandeth . . . and*"

[140] There is more to be said for the view that this is a conflation of "obey." For "obey," when interpreted causatively, would mean "cause to obey," that is, "command," and this causative is used several times by the septuagint of issuing a decree or authoritative command. Possibly, indeed, "command" alone (without "obey") stood in the original. If it did, the evangelists might feel that to "command" did not imply obedience, so that they preferred to take the causative in a non-causative meaning. In that case, Luke is here restoring the original meaning, while not venturing to reject the erroneous interpretation which is compatible with the correct one.[3]

---

[1] Fear (ירא) = φοβεῖσθαι (frequ.). The pass. particip. = θαυμαστός (6).

[2] Comp. Ezra ii. 1, "*each* (איש)," LXX ἀνήρ, but parallel 1 Esdr. v. 8 ἕκαστος. In 2 K. xi. 9 ἔλαβεν ἀνήρ means, "they *each* took," and the parallel 2 Chr. xxiii. 8 has ἕκαστος.

[3] Lk. viii. 25 "He commandeth (ἐπιτάσσει)": a full discussion of this passage would require a comparison of it with Mk. i. 27 (Lk. iv. 36), "even the unclean spirits *he commandeth*," where Mk. adds "and they *obey* him (ὑπακούουσιν αὐτῷ),"

§ 6. (*Luke*) " On the next day . . . from the mountain"

Mark ix. 9	Matt. xvii. 9	Luke ix. 36-37
"And when they were coming down from the mountain he straitly charged them that they should relate to no man. . . ."	"And when they were coming down from the mountain, Jesus commanded them saying, 'Tell no man. . . .'"	"And they were silent and reported to no man in those days . . . But it came to pass (a_1) *on the next day* when they had come down (a_2) *from the mountain.*"

(i.) *Speech or fact?*

[141] The variation of Matthew from Mark suggests that the original—as is sometimes the case (**28, 86, 240**) in Hebrew—might be interpreted "tell no man," or, "they told no man." Very possibly in early collections of the sayings of Jesus, the preface "and Jesus said" might be omitted, and then Evangelists might easily differ as Mark and Matthew do in the Institution of the Lord's Supper where Mark has "and they drank of it all (of them)," but Matthew "drink of it all [of you]."[1]

[142] Or the Hebrew original may have been "he commanded *and* they were silent," taken by Mark and Matthew to mean, as it often does, "he commanded *that* they should be silent." The synoptic divergences might then be explained if the original were "And he caused them to be silent and they reported nothing." Luke took "caused them to be silent" non-causatively, "they were silent." Mark and Matthew paraphrased it, "strictly enjoined (silence) on them."

(ii) *Luke's addition, "on the next day."*

Lk., "and they go forth." Perhaps the original of Mk. i. 27 ended at "commandeth," and the rest was added for clearness.

Mt. has no parallel to Mk. i. 27 and to its context. The Hebrew for "spirits" is also the Hebrew for "winds." Possibly "unclean" was added in Mk. i. 27 to the original for clearness. If so, Mt. may have identified (i.) "he commandeth *the spirits*" with (ii.) "he commandeth *the winds*," and may have dropped the narrative depending upon (i.). [1] Mk. xiv. 23, Mt. xxvi. 27.

[143] A new and important fact introduced by the latest of the three Evangelists must not be discarded on the mere ground of its lateness: for Luke manifestly had access to traditions not found in Mark or Matthew. But an unimportant detail like this is not antecedently likely to be derived from special tradition. Nor does it seem likely that Luke would insert it, as an inference of his own, for the sake of defining the time of the descent from the mountain.

[144] If therefore good evidence of the possibility of conflative origin can be produced, the words "on the next day" must be regarded with suspicion. Now the Hebrew for "to-morrow" is very like the Hebrew for "from the mountain," and the two are actually conflated in the Vision of Elijah, where the Hebrew is "Go forth and stand *on the mountain*," but the Septuagint, "Go forth (a_1) *on the morrow* and stand ... (a_2) *on the mountain*." Probably, then, Luke's detail is due to conflation.[1]

[1] [144*a*] 1 K. xix. 11 "on the mountain (בהר)," αὔριον (leg. מחר) (ם and ב are (158*a*) often confused). "From the mountain"=מהר, "on the morrow"=מחר.

It is possible that Lk. ix. 36 (a_1) "in *those days*," and ix. 37 (a_2) "on *the next day*," may represent two attempts to make sense out of the reading מחר. It means literally "to-morrow," but might be (wrongly) interpreted "on the following day (*i.e.* the day following a *past* day) (מחרת)," or "in the days that immediately followed."

CHAPTER II

CONFLATIONS IN THE STORY OF THE GADARENE

§ 1. *Conflative tendency apparent in Mark*

[145] When a passage contains several difficulties, all explained or corrected by marginal alternatives, it is natural that the editor, if he conflates in one instance, should conflate in the others also. He may, of course, accept some and reject others of the marginal glosses; but there is an antecedent probability that errors of this kind will "flock together." This we have found to be the case (95) in the Old Testament, and the story of the Gadarene appears to exemplify this tendency in Mark :—

(i.) (Mark v. 5), "(a_1) in *the tombs and* (a_2) in *the mountains*."

[146] Matthew and Luke mention "the tombs," but not "the mountains." The Hebrew of the two words is not similar, but they are confused in Isaiah, "thou art cast away *from thy sepulchre*"; LXX, "thou shalt be cast *on the mountains*."[1] The same verse of Mark contains—

(ii.) (Mark v. 5), "(a_1) *crying and* (a_2) *cutting (or, bruising) himself with stones*."

---

[1] [146a] Is. xiv. 19, "from thy *sepulchre* (מקברך)," ἐν τοῖς ὄρεσιν (? leg. some form of רום or הר). It is more easy to see why Mk. v. 2, "there met him *from the tombs*," is parallel to Lk. viii. 27, "there met him *from the city*" : for קריה ("city") is somewhat like קברה ("graves").

Dr. Taylor suggests, on Is. xiv. 19, Gk. corr., σόρους for ὄρεσιν. In favour of this, see Job xxi. 32 "*burial-mound* (נרש)" σωρῶν, A σορω.

[147] Matthew and Luke mention "crying," but not "cutting," or "bruising." The Hebrew "bruise," "break," etc., is one of those words most frequently mistranslated by the Septuagint. It is almost always confused with "evil" or "mischief," and the latter is confused with "cry" in Micah, "Why dost thou cry [with] crying," where the Septuagint confuses "crying" with "evil." Mark may very well have conflated (a_1) "crying," and (a_2) "doing himself a mischief," (or "bruising himself,") adding "with stones" for the sake of clearness.[1]

(iii.) The next instance occurs in two forms in Mark corresponding to one in Matthew, and apparently to one in Luke—

Mark v. 3, 4 (lit.)	Matt. viii. 28 (lit.)	Luke viii. 27 (lit.)
"Not even with a *chain* any longer was any one able to bind him, ... and no one had-power to tame him."	"No one had-power[2] to pass by that way."	"For a long time he had not put on a *garment*."

In the attempt to trace these diverging traditions to one Hebrew original we have to find reasons for the following facts :—(i.) Matthew nowhere, in this narrative, mentions "chains," or "garments"; (ii.) Luke substitutes "garment" for "chain" here, though he mentions "chains" later on; (iii.) Mark nowhere mentions the refusal to wear clothes, though he says later on that the demoniac was "clothed and in his right mind"; (iv.) Matthew alone inserts (in apparent parallelism to the "chain" or "garment"), "no man had power to pass that way."

[148] A solution would be afforded by an original to

[1] For the mistranslation of רעע "crush," see above, 7. Cp. Mic. iv. 9, "aloud, *i.e.* crying (רע)," κακά. "Cry"=רע, and "crush"=רעע.

[2] Mt. viii. 28, "had-power," ἰσχύειν, so translated in order to identify it with "had-power" in Mk. v. 4.

this effect, "he would not so much as gird himself with a girdle," that is, he would wear no clothing. For this would be, in substance, Luke's tradition. And bearing in mind the play of words in John, "another shall *gird* thee,"—referring to the binding of Peter before crucifixion—we see that "gird" might be taken in the sense of "bind."[1] Hence Mark may have taken the meaning to be "he could never be bound with bonds." But the same Hebrew root means also "strengthen," and hence the phrase might be translated "was strong enough to bind." Again, by a slight change, it would mean "go" or "pass," and the latter would give Matthew's tradition, "No one *was strong enough to pass by.*"[2]

If this is the correct explanation, Luke is nearest to the original.

(iv.) Mark v. 15	Matt. viii. 34	Luke viii. 35
"They behold the (a_1) *demoniac*, (? b_1) *seated*, (? b_2) *clothed*, (? b_3) *and in his right mind*, (a_2) *him that had had the legion.*"	"having seen him (*i.e.* Jesus)."	"they found [there] seated the man from whom the devils had gone forth, clothed, and in his right mind, by the feet of Jesus."

[149] In itself, this passage of Mark could be accepted without hesitation. But we have to explain why Matthew omitted it. And the variation of Luke from Mark—slight though it may seem—must not be overlooked. That Luke should alter Mark's "demoniac"—literally "the man-having-the-devil" (pres. particip.)—is intelligible, for he no longer had the devil. But the slight variation in the order of

---

[1] Jn. xxi. 18, explained by Tertullian and commentators generally as meaning the binding of a prisoner by executioners.

[2] [148*a*] The letter ב is frequ. confused with ר, so that אור "gird," or "bind" might be taken as אור = πορεύεσθαι. אור (Mandelk. Concord.) = "vinculum" as well as "cingulum": and the Lexicon takes it as "chain" in Job xii. 18 (but not R.V., nor LXX): אור = ἐνισχύειν, κατισχύειν, and ἰσχύειν.

the words "seated," etc., is such as often proceeds from marginal additions inserted in different places of the text. Also Mark's words (a_2) "him that had had the legion," superfluously added to (a_1) "demoniac," suggest that the original contained simply "he," and that a_1 and a_2 were subsequently added to define the pronoun, or else that a_2 was a correction made by some one who, like Luke, objected to a_1. Lastly, the prevalence of conflations in the context would make it reasonable to ask whether there is anything in the nature of the words "seated" "clothed" and "in his right mind" that points to further conflation.

The Hebrew "sit" is repeatedly confused (9) with the Hebrew "return," or "restore," which might well have originated "restored [to his right-mind]." Again, the word "clothed" is easily confused with "to return," and the last two words are actually confused in Ecclesiasticus, where the Hebrew has "to return," but the editors read "clothed," while the Septuagint has a third reading.[1] These facts, together with the considerations above mentioned, lead to the conclusion that the passage in Mark is corrupted— "clothed" and "in his right mind" being a conflation—and that Matthew omitted it on account of its corruption.

§ 2. (*Mark*) "*the country*," (*Luke*) "*the abyss*"

Mark v. 10	Matt. om.	Luke viii. 31
"And he began to beseech him much that he would not send them out of *the country*."		"And they began to beseech him that he would not command them to go away into *the abyss*."

[1] [149*a*] Sir. xl. 3: txt. לשוב, marg. לבש, above which is written לובש: LXX τεταπεινωμένου (? meaning "put to shame," leg. as from בוש). Luke himself (iv. 18 "*set at liberty* them that are bruised") adopts a confusion of a somewhat similar kind in quoting Is. lxi. 1, "bind-up (חבש)," which Luke appears to have understood as meaning "restore to freedom (חשב)": so Job v. 18 "bindeth up (חבש)" πάλιν ἀποκαθίστησιν (prob. leg. חשב).

[150] Mark's difficult phrase is omitted in the Arabic Diatessaron. The Greek word here rendered "country" means "the habitable world" in Ecclesiasticus and Isaiah.[1] Job assumes that it is a part of the punishment of the wicked to be "chased *out of the* [*habitable*] *world*"; and evil spirits, when cast out from men, are described as moving "through waterless places," that is, apart from men, and not finding rest till they return to a human tenement.[2] But, if that was the meaning of Mark's original, Mark's rendering by no means represents it. It might have been rendered "outside the world," but that would have been still obscure to a Greek reader. Hence, whereas Mark has "he besought him much that he would not send them outside the country," Luke appears to express the original meaning more clearly—though departing from Mark in grammatical form—by saying that "they [*i.e.* the evil spirits] besought him that he would not command them to go away into the abyss."

[151] Two considerations may have a bearing on Matthew's apparent omission. (i.) "From" is often (158*a*) confused in Hebrew with "in" or "into." (ii.) A negative may not improbably have been inserted or omitted in a Greek Gospel translated from Hebrew.

There are scores of such erroneous insertions, or omissions, of "not" in the Septuagint where there is no apparent excuse. But in this passage there is a special probability of the error, because the pronoun in "they besought *him*" is one of the most frequent Hebraic causes of an erroneously

---

[1] Sir. xliii. 3 "*the habitable land* (תבל)" χώραν, Is. xviii. 3 "all ye inhabitants of-the-*world* (תבל)" πάντες· ὡς χώρα κατοικουμένη (Oxf. Concord. seems wrong here, taking χώρα as = ארץ which = a *second* χώρα). In Is. vii. 19 "desolate (בתוח)," χώρας, (?) LXX leg. תבה.

[2] [150*a*] Job xviii. 18, Mt. xii. 43 (Lk. xi. 24). "Waterless," used as a noun, is a common word for "wilderness" in Hebrew; and solitary places are regarded as habitations for "wild beasts" and "satyrs," apparently terms suggesting, at least to the Greek translators of Isaiah (xiii. 21), evil spirits.

inserted Greek negative.[1] Or, on the other hand, the Hebrew negative might have been dropped by the Greek, being taken as a pronoun.

[152] But does Matthew omit this difficult tradition? May not Mark and Luke be conflating while Matthew gives a single version of what he conceives to be the original? It is impossible to answer with confidence because the discrepancies are so many and so complex; but it is a probable conjecture that some confusion underlies the different statements, in this narrative, about "beseeching *to go*," "beseeching *to send* (*i.e.* (possibly) *to cause to go*)," "beseeching *to permit to go into*," and " beseeching *not to send.*" These might be connected, positively or negatively, with "abyss," "country," "borders," and taken as referring to the home of the evil spirits, or to the habitable world, or to the "borders" of the citizens of Gerasa who subsequently (**155**) "beseech" Jesus to "go away." Again the word "abyss" in Ecclesiasticus is confused by the Septuagint with the third personal pronoun,[2] so that "into *them*" might be confused with "into *the abyss.*" These considerations suggest that conflation may underlie Mark and Luke in the following:—

Mark v. 10-12	Matth. viii. 31	Luke viii. 31-32
"Not send them *out of the country*... Send us into the swine, that *we may go into them.*"	"If thou art-to-cast us out, send us into the herd of swine."	"Not command them to go away *into the abyss*... permit them to go *into them* (*i.e.* the swine)."[3]

[**153**] It seems probable that very early difficulties

---

[1] Delitzsch gives לֹא here in Mk.-Lk.; אַל in Mt. The former is repeatedly confused with לֹא (**123***a*); the latter might be confused with the hortative negative אַל.

[2] Sir. xliii. 23:... planted islands *in-the-deep* (בתהום)," ἐφύτευσεν αὐτὴν 'Ιησοῦς, a corruption of ἐν αὐτῇ νήσους. "In them" (and often "into them") would be בהם.

[3] Lk. "them (ἐκείνους)"; Mk. "them (αὐτούς)."

would be found by Hebraic as well as by Hellenistic evangelists in the phrase above quoted about "the country"; and, owing to the special difficulty, Hebraic alternatives might be inserted in the margin, not because they resembled the letters of the original ("habitable land"), but because they appeared more fitting or less obscure. This is often the case in the Hebrew of Ecclesiasticus, and it might well be so here, where the words of the Lord are not in question. But, if this were the case, the probability of confusion would be greatly increased, and especially of confusion by conflation.

[154] The confusion between "going" and "sending," or "causing to go," might naturally arise from mistaking a causative for a non-causative form. But, further, these two forms are so similar to the Hebrew "command" or "send word," that even in Hebrew parallels there appears confusion between them. For example, where Kings tells us that Jehoiada "*commanded* the captains," Chronicles has "and (he) *brought out* the captains"; and the Greek of the latter mistranslates "brought out" first (a_1) non-causatively, as "went out," and then (a_2) as "commanded," conflating so as to produce the following result: "and he (a_1) *went out* . . . and (a_2) *commanded*." This confusion between "send" and "command" probably explains a remarkable discrepancy in the Double Traditions, where Matthew makes the centurion "come," but Luke makes him "send" to Jesus.[1]

Hence, when Mark has "that he should not send them," *i.e.* "cause them to go," and the parallel Luke has, "that he should not command them to go," it is possible that Luke may not be freely rendering the causative of "go," but may be conflating (a_1) "go" and (a_2) "command," like the Septuagint above. And the original may be either

[1] Mt. viii. 5, προσῆλθεν; Lk. vii. 3, ἀπέστειλεν. 2 K. xi. 15, "and he commanded (וַיְצַו)" = 2 Chr. xxiii. 14, "and [he] brought out (וַיּוֹצֵא)," (a_1) ἐξῆλθεν . . . (a_2) ἐνετείλατο. Comp. Judg. iii. 19, "and there went out (pl.) (וַיֵּצְאוּ)," ἐξαπέστειλεν (but A ἐξῆλθθ); Gen. l. 16, "and they sent-a-message (וַיְצַוּוּ)" καὶ παρεγένοντο.

"command," as in Kings, or "cause to go," as in Chronicles, or perhaps "go."

[155] Our conclusion is that Matthew may have omitted the clause about "sending from the country," not because he was ignorant of it, but because he regarded it as an erroneous version of a tradition that he has himself preserved in company with Mark and Luke, viz. "they [the people of Gerasa] besought him *to go away from their borders.*"[1]

Although this particular conclusion is but a conjecture, the investigation of the Mark-parallels as a whole results in a conclusion that may be described as certain, namely, that some of the details in Mark, omitted or altered by Matthew or by Luke, or by both, are the results of conflation, and must not be accepted as historical. Luke, so far, is less conflative than Mark. Matthew, where he does not follow Mark, appears the least conflative of the three.

[1] Mk. v. 17, ἀπελθεῖν (Mt. viii. 34, ὅπως μεταβῇ) ἀπὸ τῶν ὁρίων αὐτῶν, Lk. viii. 37 . . . τῆς περιχώρου τῶν Γερασηνῶν ἀπελθεῖν ἀπ' αὐτῶν.

The final ם in the Hebrew "send *them*" might be repeated as the preposition "from," thus changing "send to" into "send *from.*"

CHAPTER III

CONFUSIONS OF WORDS

§ 1. (*Mark*) "*Idumaea*," (*Matthew*) "*Syria*"

WE have seen above that Septuagint errors of confusion are often due to the similarity of the Hebrew *d* and *r;* and instances were given of the consequent confusion of "Edom" with "Aram," *i.e.* "Syria," of "know" with "shepherd," of "across" with "servant," etc. Therefore, if we are seeking to ascertain whether the Synoptic Gospels bear traces of translation from Hebrew, these words, and the others mentioned above with them as constantly interchanged in the Septuagint, ought first to engage our attention in the Gospels.

[156] We therefore begin with "Idumaea" or "Edom." Antecedently, this would seem a hopeless word. Every reader of the New Testament is aware that the old names, Edom, Moab, and Ammon, rarely, if ever, occur in its pages. In the first century Edom was called Idumaea; but the name is never used by Luke, though he mentions the less known Trachonitis, Abilene, and Ituraea. No convert is recorded as coming from it, and it is never mentioned in the Acts, Epistles, or in any Gospel but one, namely, Mark, and there only once.

[157] Naturally we turn with interest to the parallels in Matthew and Luke. But here we have to bear in mind what was said above (**16**) about the probability of modifications of the earliest Gospel by harmonisers, so that important

discrepancies arising from mistranslation would rarely survive except where the parallel contexts diverged. If Mark had written that people "came to Jesus from *Galilee, Idumaea and Judaea*" and Matthew and Luke "came to Jesus from *Galilee, Decapolis, and Judaea*," it is highly probable that the rare and quite unexpected "Idumaea" would have been altered to "Decapolis" in the first century, so that Mark's original reading would have been utterly lost. But it happens that Matthew's context varies a good deal from Mark's. It was shown (18) that Luke represents the Baptist coming *to the country* round Jordan where Matthew represents the people of that country coming *to the Baptist*. Again, it was shown (129) that the Hebrew "hearing" may mean a "report" or "fame" about a person. Hence, where Mark says "*hearing* how many [great deeds] he was doing, they came," and Luke "who came *to hear* him," we must not be surprised if Matthew has "there came the *report* about him" (lit. "his hearing"). With these preliminaries remembered, we may be prepared to recognise divergent translation from Hebrew in the following passages where Mark alone has retained the old and difficult (a_1) "Idumaea," while Matthew has (a_2) "Syria."

Mark iii. 8	Matt. iv. 24-5 (lit.)	Luke vi. 17
"... and *from* (a_1) *Idumaea* and beyond Jordan, (a_2) and *about Tyre and Sidon*, a great multitude, (b) *hearing* how many [great deeds] he was doing, came unto him."	"And there came[1] (b) *his hearing* [*i.e.* his fame spread] *into* the whole of (a_2) *Syria* ... and there followed him many crowds ... and from beyond Jordan."	"And a great crowd of his disciples, and a great multitude of the people, from ... and *from* (a_2) *the seacoast of Tyre and Sidon*, who came (b) *to hear him*."

[158] Probably Mark himself retains a trace of the reading "Syria." He might not like to say that "people came

---

[1] Mt. iv. 24, "came," lit. "came away," ἀπῆλθεν.

from Syria *and* from Galilee and from Judaea, etc.," because "Syria" *included* "Galilee and Judaea." But the meaning of "(northern) Syria" was substantially expressed by (a_3) "about Tyre and Sidon." So Mark may have conflated a_1 and a_3. Luke took a_3 alone. Matthew took a_2 alone, and avoided the hyperbolical statement that "people came hearing (or to hear) *from all Syria*" by changing it to "there came a hearing (*i.e.* a report) *into* all Syria."[1]

A great many points of interest in these parallel passages must be reserved for another occasion. The object here is simply to prove translation from Hebrew. In this and future instances space will not allow of a full answer to the question "which evangelist is closest to the original?" But thus much may be said with advantage once for all that *the difficult reading is generally the original one*; and the difficult reading here is "Idumaea."

§ 2. *The prophecy of Amos concerning* "*Edom*"

[159] It is probable that a prophecy of Amos, quoted erroneously in the Acts of the Apostles as predicting the inclusion of the Gentiles in the Church, was the basis of Mark's tradition. The original mentioned "Edom" and the nations "called by the name" of Jehovah.[2] The latter might be taken as meaning the different parts of Palestine. These, accordingly, Mark (iii. 7) adds to "Edom." But in the Acts, "Edom"—which in Hebrew is identical with "Adam" (both being *a'dm*)—is regarded as referring to "man" gener-

---

[1] [158*a*] For "from" (-מ) confused with "in" (-ב), see 2 Chr. xxv. 23 (lit.) "*in* (-ב) the wall ... *from* (-מ) the gate," ἀπὸ ... ἀπὸ ... =2 K. xiv. 13 "*in* ... *in*" ἐν ... ἐν: 2 Chr. xxv. 27, "conspired against him *in* Jerusalem and he fled to Lachish," ἐπέθεντο αὐτῷ ἐπίθεσιν καὶ ἔφυγεν ἀπὸ 'Ι. εἰς Λ.; 2 Chr. xxiii. 20 "from the house of the Lord," εἰς οἶκον K. See **9***a* and **144***a*.

[2] Amos ix. 12: "That they may possess the remnant of *Edom* and all the nations which are called by my name," quoted by James in Acts xv. 17, thus, "that the residue of *men* may seek after the Lord, and all the Gentiles upon whom my name is called"—correctly from the LXX, which, however, is erroneous.

ally. That shows at how very early a period the mention of "Edom" was likely to cause variations and to give rise to confusion with "Aram," *i.e.* "Syria," and to conflations such as "the sea coast of Tyre and Sidon."

[160] These considerations may prepare the way for a second rule, if it is seen to be supported by further experience. *A difficult reading, found in Mark alone, will derive additional probability from evidence indicating that it may be based on the language of prophecy.*[1]

§ 3. (*Matthew*) "*perfect*," (i.) (*Mark and Luke*) "*lacking*" *or* "*wanting*," (ii.) (*Luke*) "*compassionate*."

[161] This, like the last instance, will be found to involve a confusion of *d* and *r;* the word *chsd* means "compassionate," "saintly," and hence, by a free paraphrase, "perfect." The word *chsr* means "lacking" or "wanting." The second parallel may be conveniently taken first:

Matth. v. 48.	Luke vi. 36.
"Be ye therefore *perfect* as your Father in heaven is *perfect*."	"Become *compassionate* as your Father in heaven is *compassionate*."

[162] Among the Jews, the name for "a Saint" was "a merciful [one]," *Chasid*. Jesus bade His disciples become "saints," not after the pattern of the Pharisees, but after the pattern of the Father in heaven, who is beneficent to all. This Matthew expressed freely by "perfect," Luke more literally, but not so faithfully to the spirit of the utterance, by "compassionate."

So far, there is no error, nothing but the difference

---

[1] Mark in his own person perhaps never *quotes* prophecy. But his language, like that of any early evangelist, might naturally be based upon prophecy, or contain allusions to it. In Mk. i. 2 the prophecy may have been originally intended as an utterance of John the Baptist.

CONFUSIONS OF WORDS [165]

between a broad and a narrow rendering. But the following contains error :—

Mark x. 21.	Matth. xix. 21.	Luke xviii. 22.
"One thing is *lacking* to thee."	"If thou desirest to be perfect."	"Yet one thing *is wanting* to thee."

[163] The Hebrew for the Greek "lacking" is thrice חסר (*chsr*) in the Septuagint, and this is actually confused with חסד (*chsd*) in Proverbs, "He knoweth not that *want* shall come upon him"; LXX, "he knoweth not that *the merciful* shall have power upon him."[1]

[164] The original was probably, as in Matthew, "Is it in thy mind (Heb. soul) to become a saint?" But (i.) "thy mind (or, soul)" is repeatedly rendered "thee" by the Septuagint; (ii.) the word "in" might easily be confused with "one thing"; (iii.) "Saint" was confused with "lacking." The three causes resulted in (Mark) "(ii.) one thing (iii.) is lacking (i.) to thee." Luke, whom we have found above objecting to Matthew's word "perfect," followed Mark's error.[2]

§ 4. (*Mark and Matthew*) "*on foot*," *an error*[2]

[165] In the following passage, immediately before the "Feeding of the Five Thousand," it can be shown that there is antecedent probability that Mark (followed in part by Matthew) has made a mistake avoided by Luke.

Mark vi. 33.	Matth. xiv. 13.	Luke ix. 11.
". . . ran together there *on foot* from all the cities and came before them."	". . . *followed* him on foot from the cities."	". . . *followed* him."

[1] Prov. xxviii. 22, the Heb. is חסר (LXX leg. חסד): the *Oxf. Conc.*, by error, gives חסד. Another confusion of חסר (in a different sense) with חסד occurs in Prov. xiv. 34 "is-a-reproach (חסד)," ἐλασσονοῦσι.

[2] Comp. Gen. xxiii. 8 "If it is *in* (את) your mind . . ." "One thing" = אחת which is easily confused with את, *i.e.* "with," or "in."

101

CONFUSIONS OF WORDS

Here Mark says that people ran together "on foot" from "all the cities" and reached the point aimed at before those who went with Jesus in the boat. (i.) It is in the highest degree unlikely that people "on foot" could thus anticipate twelve able-bodied men in a boat. Anyone who has experienced the difference of time between passing on land, or by boat, from one point of, say Derwentwater, or Ullswater, will recognise this. (ii.) Matthew and Luke both omit Mark's statement that the multitudes reached the place first, and both say that the people "followed" Jesus.

[166] The explanation is very simple. Mark has misunderstood the Hebraic "at *his* feet," *i.e.* at the feet of Jesus, and has taken it to mean "with *their* feet." The error is a very natural one and occurs repeatedly (**75-76**) in the Septuagint, *e.g.* "And the king went forth *and all his household after him*," LXX "and all his household *on their feet*."[1] In another passage, "the people *that follow me*" is rendered by the Septuagint "the people *that are my footsoldiers*," but by Aquila literally "the people that is in my feet."[2]

Matthew conflates "followed" with "on foot." Luke gives the correct rendering.

§ 5. (*Mark and Matthew*) "*in the* (or, *a*) *boat to a desert place.*" (*Luke*) "*to a city called Bethsaida.*"

Mark vi. 32	Matt. xiv. 13	Luke ix. 10
"In the boat to a desert place."	"In a boat to a desert place."	"To a city called Bethsaida."

[167] "Bethsaida" means "House of Provision."[3] Luke

---

[1] 2 S. xv. 16-18, "at his feet," *i.e.* "following him," is there twice translated "with their feet (τοῖς ποσὶν αὐτῶν)," and once πεζῇ.
[2] 1 K. xx. 10.
[3] "Provision (ציד) "=(11) ἐπισιτισμός, used here by Luke (Lk. ix. 12, "Send away the multitudes that they may go into the villages and fields round about and find *provision*"), and nowhere else in N.T.

alone connects it here with the Feeding of the Five Thousand. Later on, where Mark and Matthew have "that they may buy themselves *something to eat*, or, *food*," Luke alone has "provision." In the historical books of the Septuagint the Greek "provision" occurs ten times, but in the whole of the Prophets and Psalms *only once*, and there in a passage that may well have seemed to the earliest Christians appropriate to Christ as the Shepherd of Israel feeding the flock in the wilderness: "Men did eat the bread of *the mighty* (A.V. and LXX *angels*); he sent them *provision* to the full." The Psalmist's immediately preceding words, "He gave them of the corn of heaven," are quoted by John in connection with the Five Thousand.[1] It may be taken as certain that when Luke used the name "Bethsaida" and the word "provision," he had in mind the unique instance in which the word is used in the Psalms, and regarded the name as appropriate to the miracle. If so, he would naturally be prejudiced in favour of any variation of the text of Mark that allowed him to substitute his tradition in the place of Mark's.

[168] Now the Greek language is deficient as compared with Hebrew in words that express different kinds of wildernesses and deserts. In one passage of Jeremiah the single Greek word used here by Mark and Matthew expresses three Hebrew words.[2] Here the original for "desert" may have been the word employed by the Psalmist (Ps. lxiii. 1), "O God, my God, early will I seek thee in a *dry* and weary land where no water is"; where the Septuagint uses Mark's word "desert" to represent "dry." But "Place-of-Drought" (*bthtzih*) is very like "Place-of-Provision" (*bthtzidh*).

[169] Next, to explain Luke's "city." We have seen (12, 13, 73) that *Arabah*, "wilderness," is easily confused with a word meaning "ferry-boat." Now *Arabah* is confused with "city" in Joshua, "to the *plains* (lit. *Araboth*) of Jericho";

---

[1] Ps. lxxviii. 24, 25, Jn. vi. 31.   [2] Jer. l. 12.

LXX "the *city* of Jericho."[1] If, therefore, the original described how the Messiah went forth into "an Arabah, a place-of-drought," there is precedent for supposing that Luke may have corrupted "Arabah" into "city." We have also seen above that a striking similarity of letters justifies the belief that he may have corrupted "place-of-drought" into "Bethsaida." The two corruptions would convert "Arabah a place of drought" into "city Bethsaida."

[170] Luke's mention of Bethsaida has given geographers and commentators a great deal of trouble, because the context seemed to necessitate a city on the west of the lake. That difficulty might be surmounted more easily than the following objections :—(i.) There seems an absurdity in the supposition that the disciples, being in, or quite near, a populous and prosperous city like Bethsaida, should say, "send the multitudes *away* to buy provision"; (ii.) There is a contradiction, which has never been satisfactorily explained, between the "desert" of Mark and Matthew, and the "city" of Luke. If the meaning were "the desert round the city," the hungry multitudes would be sent to buy food in the *city*. But they are sent to the surrounding "farms and villages!" All these difficulties vanish if Luke's "Bethsaida" is a mere corruption of "desert."

§ 6. *Was "boat" in the Original?*

The introduction of a "boat" harmonises very well—antithetically and on paper—with the notion that the multitudes went round "on foot." But, if linguistic and practical considerations show that "on foot" is a mistake, the question arises whether "by boat" may not be a mistake too.

[171] We have seen above in discussing the variations

---

[1] Josh. iv. 13, "plains (ערבות)," "city"=עיר: "a″r-bth-tzdh"="city Bethsaida"; "a″rbh tzih"="dry desert."

of Beth*abara*, "the place of a ferry-boat or ford," and Beth*araba*, "a place in the wilderness," that the two words "boat" and "wilderness" might easily be interchanged. And here "wilderness" is the more probable for the following reasons :—

Mark frequently mentions a boat where the other evangelists do not, and sometimes he appears to be wrong. Also Mark is unquestionably wrong in the context where he describes the multitude as going "on foot," and this increases the probability that he is wrong here. John follows Luke in mentioning no boat.[1] Having regard to the Hebraic habit of accumulating words such as "wilderness," "dry place," "solitary place," etc., contrary to the genius of Greek, it is antecedently probable that the original would use two synonymous words here, and that the Greek translators would be disposed to find a new meaning for one of them.

§ 7. *The earthquake recorded by Matthew alone*

[172] After saying that "Jesus uttered a great cry and expired," Mark mentions the rending of the veil of the temple and then passes to what the centurion said. Luke, with some variation of order, does the same. Matthew, between the rending of the veil and the words of the centurion, inserts a description of an "earthquake" to which he refers in the following passage, parallel to passages of Mark and Luke which make no mention of it :—

[1] [171*a*] Jn. vi. 1, "After these things [*i.e.* Christ's acts in Jerusalem] Jesus went away beyond the sea of Galilee, the [sea of] Tiberias." Starting from Jerusalem Jesus might go through the southern part of Decapolis. Comp. Mark's description of Christ's journey before the Feeding of the Four Thousand (Mk. vii. 31). "And again he went out from the borders of Tyre, and came through Sidon *unto* the sea of Galilee *through the midst of the borders of Decapolis*," where Mt. xv. 29 has "he went *along* (παρά) the sea of Galilee." It would be quite natural to infer from Jn.'s words that Jesus crossed the lake by boat. But the inference would be by no means certain.

CONFUSIONS OF WORDS

Mark xv. 39	Matth. xxvii. 54	Luke xxiii. 47
"But the centurion, having seen . . . that he thus *expired*, said . . ."	"But the captain of the hundred and those with him . . . having seen *the earthquake* and the things *that were coming to pass*, feared exceedingly, saying . . ."	"But the captain of the hundred, having seen *that which had come to pass*, glorified God, saying . . ."

[173] The versions of Mark given by Codex Bezae and the Syro-Sinaitic, instead of conforming Mark's brief account to that of Matthew or Luke, rather suggest a confusion of "expire" with "exclaim" and a consequent conflation. But the confused nature of the traditions followed by the former is indicated by the fact that, in Luke, it makes the *centurion* "call out."

Mark (Codex Bezae)
". . . having seen him thus *exclaiming* and [that] he *expired*."

Luke (Codex Bezae)
"And the captain of the hundred, *having called out*, glorified God, saying . . ."

Mark (Syro-Sinaitic)
". . . saw him *exclaiming* and *expiring*."

These variations suggest some confusion arising from a similarity between the Hebrew of "exclaim," "come to pass," and possibly "earthquake" and "fear."

[174] Delitzsch gives, as the modern Hebrew translation of Luke's "that which *had come to pass*," the passive participle of the verb "do."[1] This, as there is no past participle, might be translated by Matthew "the things that *were coming to pass*." On the other hand, Mark might take it as meaning

---

[1] Niph. of נעשׂה. "Cry out (שׁוע)" (Ps. xviii. 41) is interchanged (parall. 2 S. xxii. 42) with שׁוע, which is confused with נעשׂה, "do," in Ex. v. 9. Trommius also suggests that שׁוע and נעשׂה are confused in 1 K. xx. 40.

"that which *he* (*i.e.* Jesus) *did*"—the verb "do" being used in Hebrew as in English to avoid the repetition of a verb. But if a translator took it thus, the necessities of Greek idiom might induce him to substitute for the general verb "do" the particular verb of action. For example, in Genesis, where God is represented in the Hebrew text, as saying "I will not *do it*"—that is "I will not destroy," referring to a previous mention of destroying—the Greek has "I will not destroy."[1]

[175] If that was the case, translators of the present passage might take different views of the action implied by "do." Some might refer it as Mark does to the action last mentioned, namely, "expiring"; others, to the loud cry that took place at the moment of death. The latter might substitute "exclaiming." It so happens that one Hebrew word meaning "exclaim" resembles the Hebrew "do," so that—apart from the Greek objection to the Hebrew use of "do"—corruption of the Hebrew text might account for the introduction of the reading "exclaim." Again, the Hebrew "saw *that* he [Jesus] exclaimed (or, called out)," might easily be confused with "saw *and* he [the centurion] called out," and this would account for the reading of Codex Bezae in Luke.

[176] But, when the action was transferred to the centurion instead of Jesus, there would be a tendency to substitute other verbs, similar to "cry out" but more appropriate, such as "feared exceedingly," or "was greatly moved." Such a word is found in the recently recovered Hebrew of Ecclesiasticus, where the Septuagint has "The countries *wondered-greatly-at* thee," but the Hebrew "thou *didst-greatly-move* the nations," and the editors add "(lit.) *move as with a tempest*"; and the same word, in Kings, describes the "sore trouble" of the king of Syria. But this "moving" is much more often used literally, to mean a "tempest," and is then translated by the Greek word "shaking," here

---

[1] Gen. xviii. 29-30.

used by Matthew to denote an earthquake.[1] Thus, by Hebrew corruption, "he cried out" might become "there was a shaking," *i.e.* an earthquake.

Hebrew corruption could not, of course, explain Matthew's preceding details about the earthquake. But we have seen (**106-9**) in the story of Araunah, that a slight Hebrew corruption may originate an erroneous tradition, which may be subsequently amplified with a view to clearness and consistency.[2]

[**177**] It is quite possible that Codex Bezae approximates to Mark's original tradition, and that, owing to the similarity between the two words "come to pass" and "cry out," one of them dropped out in our Mark, which retained only the former, paraphrasing it as "expired." But these and other details must be left uncertain. However, all the phenomena converge to the conclusion that these remarkable Synoptic variations may be caused by translation from Hebrew, and that Matthew's "earthquake" may have originated in Hebrew corruption.

§ 8. *Peter "sitting" or "standing" during the three denials?*[3]

The Synoptists, in commencing the story of Peter's denials, describe him as "sitting," John describes him as "standing." Why is this?

[**178**] The Hebrew "sit" means also "remain" or "continue." When the Septuagint writes, "He *sat* three years and there was no war," the Hebrew is, "They *continued* three years without war."[4] The Hebrew Law of the

---

[1] "Tempest" = σεισμός or συσσεισμός, = רעש (or רעד). The verb סער =(Sir. xlvii. 17) ἀπεθαύμασαν, and (2 K. vi. 11) ἐξεκινήθη.

[2] [**176a**] Errors springing from consistency form a large class. The following is an instance on a small scale, Judg. vi. 16, "*the Lord* said," LXX "*the angel of the Lord* said." Having made this alteration, the LXX is forced subsequently to alter "*I* will be with thee" into "*the Lord* will be with thee."

[3] Mk. xiv. 54; Mt. xxvi. 58; Lk. xxii. 55; Jn. xviii. 18.

[4] 1 K. xxii. 1.

Sabbath said, "*Abide ye* every man in his place," but the Greek said, "Ye shall *sit* each one in (lit. to) your houses," and Origen's comment is, "no man can *sit* a whole day."[1] Hence, when Mark says, "I *was* daily in the temple with you teaching," and the parallel Matthew has "I *sat* daily," we perceive that Matthew is giving the literal meaning ("sit"), and Mark the real meaning ("be," or "remain.")[2]

The same applies to Mark elsewhere, "While Peter *was* below in the courtyard," (Matthew) "But Peter *sat* without in the courtyard," (Luke) "seated." There are five passages in the Septuagint, where the Greek "was," "is," etc., represents a Hebrew "sit" or "continue."[3] It is reasonable to infer that Mark's "was" represents an original Hebrew "sit," translated literally by Matthew and Luke.

[179] Although the error of Matthew and Luke was not a serious one, it may well have seemed to John important enough to be corrected. It was an error of fact, representing the officers and servants, who were standing on duty, as "sitting." It was also unseemly that the Apostle should be "sitting" while his Lord was standing on His trial. Hence it is, perhaps, that John, in his correction, instead of using the word "remain," repeatedly employs the word "stand." It is Luke that mainly needed correction. Mark mentions "sitting" only once. But Luke says that "they *sat* together ... and Peter *sat* in the midst of them," and that a servant saw him "*seated.*" John says, "the servants were *standing* ... and Peter was with them *standing*," and, again, "Now Simon Peter was *standing*."[4]

---

[1] Ex. xvi. 29; Orig., *De Princip.*, iv. 1 (Clark's Transl., vol. i. p. 319).
[2] Mk. xiv. 49; Mt. xxvi. 55.
[3] Mk. xiv. 66, Mt. xxvi. 69, Lk. xxii. 56. Gen. xxix. 14; Josh. xxiv. 7; 1 S. vii. 2; Jer. xxxviii. 7; Ezek. iii. 15.
[4] [179a] Lk. xxii. 55, 56; Jn. xviii. 18, 25. The difference may throw light upon descriptions of Jesus as "standing," or "sitting," at "the right hand of God." Both may, in the original, mean simply "abiding for ever." Verbal differences like these, springing from one and the same Hebrew original, and

§ 9. *Peter warming himself at the light* [*of a fire*]

Mark xiv. 54	Matt. xxvi. 58	Luke xxii. 55, 56
[**180**] "And he was sitting . . . and warming himself at the light [of a fire]."	". . . sat to see the end."	"but having kindled a fire around[1] . . . but seeing him seated at the light [of the fire]."

[**181**] With this must be compared—Jn. xviii. 18 : " The servants . . . were standing [there], having made a fire of charcoal, for there was a frost, and they warmed themselves; and Peter, too, was with them, standing and warming himself."[2]

(i.) (*Mark and Luke*) "*at the light*," (*Matthew*) "*to see the end*."[3]

[**182**] The Greek "light" would not refer to "fire," unless a writer introduces, as Luke is careful to do, some previous mention of a fire as being "kindled," "lit," etc. Mark makes no such mention, and hence it is reasonable to

passing into the traditional language of the Western Churches (so as to appear even in the Acts and the Epistles) may have given rise to plausible, but baseless, theological distinctions.

[1] [180*a*] Lk. xxii. 55, "having kindled around (περιάψαντες)." But around what? L. and S. give no instance of this use of the word except in the Epistles of Phalaris, Ep. v. p. 28, presumably about the fire *kindled round* the brazen bull ! Luke's use of it here has never been explained.

Instead of saying that Peter followed (as Mk.) "inside (ἔσω)" into the courtyard, Luke has μέσῳ, and again μέσος, "*in the midst* of them." He seems to wish to describe Peter as *compassed round* by tempters. Comp. *Actus Petri cum Simone* (ed. Lips. p. 54) where Peter says, as the reason for his denials, "for there were evil dogs that had *compassed me round*" (no doubt with allusion to Ps. xxii. 16, " dogs have *compassed* me.")

[2] [181*a*] For the explanation of the discrepancy between "standing" and "sitting," see last section. The Arabic Diatessaron gets rid of it by substituting "rose" for "stand" thus : "And the servants and the soldiers *rose* and made a fire in the court . . . and when the fire burned up they *sat down* round it."

[3] " At the light," πρὸς τὸ φῶς. The Hebr. for φῶς, אור, according to pointing, means " flame " or " light." " See " is " ראה."

conclude that the author (whether oral or scribal) of Mark's original Greek meant "light" in the ordinary sense, and most probably "day-light." The Hebrew "(day)light" is identical with the Hebrew "flame": and that would account for an erroneous inference, adopted by our Mark (**325***a*), that it was a fire, near which (he adds) Peter was "warming himself."

[**183**] "Light" makes excellent sense. The Jewish Law forbade a criminal trial to take place by night. The Sanhedrin might evade this by pretending that they were merely collecting evidence before daybreak; but they would not venture to begin the formal trial till the sun had risen.

This harmonises with what was proved in the previous section; that Peter was not "sitting," but "remaining" in the sense of "*waiting*," *that is, waiting for the verdict.* But according to Jewish Law this was identical with "*waiting for day-light.*" And that was the meaning of the original.

[**184**] But the Hebrew "light" or "flame" also means "enlighten," "kindle," "spectacle"; and it is very similar in some forms to the Hebrew "see," with which it is once confused in Proverbs, "*the light of* the eyes," where the Septuagint has "*the seeing* eye."[1] Hence it was easy for one evangelist to find "at *the light* [of a fire]" where another found "to *see*," and where probably the original was "toward, or for, the *daylight*."

[**185**] This may be regarded as so probable as to approach certainty. Other details are matters of conjecture. For example, whence came "the frost" mentioned by John alone? Did he supply it as an inferential detail to explain why the men lit the fire (just as Mark probably supplied "warming himself" in order to show that he assumed the "light" to be fire-light)? This might seem a sufficient explanation if we did not find that the Septuagint of Job once substitutes "frost" for "light"; and a longer form of

[1] Prov. xv. 30.

"light" might thus mean "from (or, because of) frost."[1] Matthew, having taken the erroneous view that the original meant "to see," might naturally supply "the end": and this may be accepted as a temporary hypothesis.[2]

§ 10. (*Mark*) "*come*," (*Matthew*) "*light*," (*Luke*) "*kindle*"

Mark iv. 21   Matt. v. 15   Luke viii. 16
"Nor doth the   "Nor do [men]   "But no one
lamp *come* . . ."   *light* a lamp . . ."   having *kindled* a
                                        lamp . . ."

[186] In the causative form "come" and "light" are slightly similar.[3] Possibly the original was "Doth [one] cause a lamp to come," and Mark mistook the causative. Later evangelists accepted a correction right as to the causative, but wrong as to the word. In any case the divergence points to translation from Hebrew, and a similar error occurs in Exodus, "Yet it *gave-light* by night" where the Septuagint has "The night *passed* (lit. *came* through)."[4]

§ 11. *Matthew's use of "companion!"*

[187] The Greek word "companion," when used in the vocative, is constantly applied, in light and playful irony, to those who have made themselves ridiculous. *No instance*

---

[1] [185*a*] Job xxxviii. 24: "the light (אור)" πάχνη. What Hebrew word the LXX read is very doubtful. Consistently with this error, מאור "light" would be interpreted "because of frost" and might be conflated with the "kindling of a fire."

[2] [185*b*] "End"=נצח, which in old MSS. would be practically identical with נצג: נצג might be confused with נצי which=(2) ἐμπυρίζειν "burn," (7) ἀνάπτειν "kindle."

[3] "Cause-to-come," *i.e.* bring=הביא: "kindle," "light,"=האיר.

[4] [186*a*] Ex. xiv. 20: "And it gave light (ויאר)"; LXX, καὶ διῆλθεν (? leg. some form of בוא. More probably, perhaps, LXX read עבר (the regular rendering of διέρχεσθαι), by interchange of א and y).

has been alleged from Greek literature to associate it with stern reproof.[1]

[188] (i.) But in Matthew a master addresses thus a man whom he is rebuking for an "evil eye," and a king uses the word to one whom he is on the point of having "bound hand and foot and cast out into outer darkness."[2] The two passages are peculiar to Matthew, so that we have not, in either of these instances, the advantage of a parallel Gospel. But (i.) the non-Greek use of "companion" makes it probable that Matthew is translating some Hebrew word that does (among other meanings) denote "companion," but without the playful significance attached to it in Greek. (ii.) In Hebrew, the letters meaning "companion" are identical with those meaning "bad" or "evil," and the two are repeatedly confused. In Proverbs, alone, the confusion occurs four times, and in one case the Authorised Version goes wrong. The literal translation plays on the double meaning of the word thus: "A man of *companions* [makes them] *to-the-doing-of-evil-to-himself.*" The Revised Version has, "He that maketh many friends [doeth it] *to his own destruction*"; but the Authorised, "A man [that hath] friends *must show himself friendly.*"[3]

[189] (ii.) Matthew alone says that Jesus, when arrested, said to Judas, "*Companion*, (lit.) that for which thou art present." Masses of theological comment and discourse have been written on the assumption that Jesus used these words alluding to a passage where the Psalmist complains of ill

---

[1] [187a] Comp. Plutarch ii. 158D, 1072E; Lucian, vol. i. p. 39, Nigrin. § 1, and Wetst. on Mt. xx. 13, quoting Galen, who uses the word about people previously described as "foolish."

[2] Mt. xx. 13, xxii. 12; xxvi. 50 requires special consideration (189).

[3] Prov. xviii. 24 (om. by LXX) איש רעים להתרועע. Other instances are Prov. xix. 6, "a *friend*"; LXX, "the *evil* man": Ezek. xxii., 12 "of thy *neighbour*"; LXX, "of wickedness": Ps. xv. 4, "to his own *hurt*"; LXX, "to his *neighbour*" (R.V. marg. some ancient authorities "to his friend"). Comp. Prov. vi. 3, 24; Prov. xxiv. 8; Hos. iii. 1; Ezek. xxii. 12.

treatment from his own "familiar friend."[1] If that was the original Hebrew, Matthew has mistranslated it by using "companion" (instead of "friend," or some other word that would not convey the impression of playful reproof).

[190] But in view of the fact that Mark — whom Matthew follows in the context—omits these words, we are forced to hesitate about accepting them. Yet their obscurity, and the apparent incompleteness of the sentence, make it almost certain that Matthew is attempting to give a literal translation of a Hebrew original. Matthew's word "present" is rare in the Bible. In the New Testament it occurs only here. In the Old Testament it represents once the Hebrew "*make haste.*"[2]

[191] This reminds us of John's version of Christ's last words to Judas, "What thou art doing *do quickly.*" The words resemble a phrase of warning to a self-willed man used by Epictetus "*Do as you are doing*, not even a god can save you."[3] Besides making good sense, it would also agree with the Johannine version, if we supposed that the original of the passage under discussion was " *The evil* thou art bent on doing to thyself do with speed." The Hebrew for "do-evil-to-thyself," might be mistaken for "companion," very nearly as our Authorised Version has mistaken the verb in the passage quoted above. In any case, judged by any reasonable standard derived from Greek literature, Matthew's "companion" is a mistake.[4]

[1] Ps. xli. 9.
[2] Mt. xxvi. 50, Ἑταῖρε, ἐφ' ᾧ πάρει : Deut. xxxii. 35 "make haste," πάρεστιν.
[3] Epict. iv. 9, 18 (comp. iii. 9, 8).
[4] [191a] If this explanation is correct, and if the words in John xiii. 27 are derived from the same tradition as these in Matthew, we should expect in John, not "do," but "do evil." Yet how could a tradition survive that represented Jesus as saying to Judas "do evil"? It was sure to be misrepresented by controversialists, and therefore almost sure to be altered (not in the spirit but in the letter) by evangelists. Besides, the disciples are regarded as overhearing Christ's words and as thinking that the "doing" referred to some kind of ministration,

§ 12. (*Mark*) "*wild beasts,*" (*Matthew and Luke*) "*he hungered*"

In this, and in a few later instances, specimens will be given of discrepancies arising from the confusion of an unfamiliar Hebrew word which has been corrupted into a familiar one. The following passages relate to Christ's Temptation :—

Mark i. 13.	Matth. iv. 1-2.	Luke iv. 1-2.
"And he was in the wilderness forty days, being tempted by Satan, *and he was with the wild beasts,* and the angels were ministering to him."	" . . . into the wilderness to be tempted by the devil. And, having fasted forty days and forty nights, *afterwards he hungered.*"	" . . . in the wilderness forty days, being tempted by the devil; and he ate nothing in those days, and *when they were completed he hungered.*"

[192]. The most appropriate Hebrew for "wild beasts" in a "wilderness"—associated with mention of Satan and suggestive of Christ's words about "the power of the enemy"—is a word rendered by the Septuagint once "wild beasts," once "apparitions," and once "demons."[1] The word is very rare (ציים) and closely resembles one that is very common (צום). The latter means "fast."

so that, according to that tradition, the "doing" could not have been "evil-doing."

[191*b*] Perhaps John found variations in the Hebrew Gospel, such as, for example, the LXX found in Ex. xxxii. 22 "set on *evil* (ברע)," ὅρμημα (leg. עברה by transposition). But the reader knows by this time (5) that ר is always liable to be corrupted to ד, and עבד = " do."

[1] Lk. x. 19 "Behold I have given you authority to tread upon serpents and scorpions and over all *the power of the enemy.*" Comp. Ps. xci. 13 : " Thou shalt tread upon *the lion and adder.*" [Note that Ps. xci. 11-12 is quoted by Satan in Matthew's (and Luke's) description of the Temptation.] In Acts xxviii. 4, 5, " wild beast (θηρίον)" means " serpent," and Job Testam. § 42, compared with § 41, shews that θηρίον means Satan. Meaning "beasts of the desert," ציים = Is. xiii. 21 θηρία, Is. xxxiv. 14 δαιμόνια, Jer. l. 39 ἰνδάλματα.

[193] To complete the case for translation it must be shewn that "with" (in "*with* the wild beasts") could easily be confused with Matthew's "afterwards" (Luke "when they were completed"). The two Hebrew words are somewhat similar, and are actually confused by the Septuagint in at least one passage; "*with* that which the Lord hath given"; LXX, "*after* the Lord had delivered."[1]

[194] The very early sect called the Paulicians taught that Jesus did *not* fast during the forty days, being supported by communion with the Father.[2] This appears to have been Mark's view, for he says that "the angels were ministering (*imperf.*) to him."

[195] The Greek imperfect "*were* ministering" may also mean, where the sense requires it, "*began to* minister." And Matthew gives quite a different aspect to the matter by inserting the clause about the angels (only without the definite article) after mention of "fasting" for forty days and being "hungered," and after three temptations, one being to turn stones into bread. In this new context Matthew's Greek, though identical with Mark's, has a new meaning, "angels *began to minister* unto him." Which view is erroneous is not a question that can be fully discussed here, though the facts, so far, seem decidedly to

---

[1] [193*a*] 1 S. xxx. 23:—"With"=את; "after(wards)"=אחר. Comp. Is. xliv. 24-5, "*with* me (אתי)" ἕτερος; the context is doubtful, and possibly the LXX may have paraphrased "who [is] *with me* [as a rival]" as meaning, in effect, "what *other* [is there like me]?" And this may apply to 1 S. xiv. 13 (*bis*), "after him," once ὀπίσω αὐτοῦ, but once μετ' αὐτοῦ. Error might also arise in Greek tradition from (245) confusion of μετά with gen. and accus., illustrated by Ex. xxiii. 2—"*after* a multitude," μετὰ πλειόνων, Gen. xxviii. 4, Num. xviii. 19, "to thee and thy seed *with thee*," μετά σε.

An original Greek tradition μετα θηριων may have been corrected (from Hebrew) into μετα το(υ) (?) νηστευσε (*i.e.*, νηστεῦσαι), and this into μετὰ τάδε ἐνήστευσε. For a possible confusion between "after" and "afterwards," comp. 2 Chr. xxxv. 14, "And *afterwards* they prepared," LXX "and *after they had* (μετὰ τὸ) prepared . . . ," but parallel 1 Esdr. i. 12 "but *afterwards* (μετὰ δὲ ταῦτα) they prepared."

[2] See Mr. Conybeare's edition of the Paulician "*Key of Truth*," p. 80.

favour Mark. But the point now is, that the parallelism between "wild beasts" and "fasting" is to be explained by *some* error in translating from Hebrew.

§ 13. *The healing of the paralytic:* (*Mark*) "*by four*" (*Matthew and Luke*) "*on a bed*"

Mark ii. 3-5.	Matth. ix. 2.	Luke v. 18-20.
"And [people] come bringing unto him a paralytic *carried by four* [And, not being able . . .] And Jesus, seeing their faith, . . ."	"And behold they brought to him a paralytic *prostrate on a bed*. And Jesus, seeing their faith . . ."	"And behold men bringing *on a bed* a man that was paralysed [. . . and not finding . . .]. And Jesus, seeing their faith."

The brackets in Mark and Luke represent a description, omitted by Matthew, of the letting down of the paralytic by his friends through *an opening in the roof*, an action of strenuous and trustful effort that gives special force to the words "seeing their faith." Antecedently it seems improbable that Matthew would have omitted this if he had known it and had believed it to be correct. It is suggested and maintained in the following remarks that a Hebrew word meaning "opening in the roof" is latent in the Synoptists under the words "four" and "bed," and that the Hebrew original was "(i.) hoisted in (ii.) at the trap-door-in-the-roof."

[196] (i.) The Hebrew "hoist," "suspend"—twice translated in the Septuagint by the word here used by Mark—is replaced in Chronicles by the much more common word "stretch." Matthew has probably made the same substitution, and has taken the word to mean "stretched [helplessly on a sick bed]," which exactly suited his context "on a bed." Luke, possibly taking the same view, may have omitted the word as superfluous.[1]

[1] "Hoist"=נטל, which=(2) αἴρω. It is interchanged with the much more common נטה "stretch," in 2 S. xxiv. 12, 1 Chr. xxi. 10. The latter=(2) αἴρω (1) βάλλω (1) ἐπιβάλλω.

(ii.) "*The trap-door in the roof*": (*a*) *suggested by Mark's text*
In order to understand this point, we must compare the details given by Mark and Luke, but omitted by Matthew:—

Mark ii. 4. (R.V.)	Luke v. 19 (R.V.)
[197] "And when they could not come nigh unto him for the crowd, they uncovered (ἀπεστέγασαν) the roof (στέγην) where he was; and, when they had broken it up.¹ . . .	"And not finding by what [way] they might bring him in because of the multitude, they went up to the house-top, and let him down through the tiles . . .

[198] The word here translated "roof" by the Revised Version (and frequently used thus in classical Greek), though used elsewhere by Matthew and Luke in the phrase "under my roof," means, radically, "covering"; and the Septuagint uses it thus when it speaks of (literally) "the *covering* of my rafters," where the Hebrew has "shadow" and we might say "the shelter of my roof." So, too, Noah is said to have (R.V.) "removed the *covering* of the Ark and looked."²

[199] The regular Greek word for "roof," found in the LXX twenty-seven times and in the New Testament seven times, is the one employed by Luke here and translated by the Revised Version "house-top"; and the fact that Mark uses a different word here suggests that he may not have

¹ [197*a*] "Broken it up," ἐξορύξαντες, a scarcely justifiable rendering (202). To express "making a hole in the roof," Thucydides has (iv. 48) διελόντες τὴν ὀροφήν.

² [198*a*] Mark's word rendered by R.V. "roof," στέγη, occurs twice as transl. of Hebr. in LXX: Gen. viii. 13, "the *covering*" (Aqu. κάλυμμα); Gen. xix. 8, "the *shadow* of my roof," τὴν στέγην τῶν δοκῶν μου. It occurs in New Testament only here, and in Mt. viii. 8, = Lk. vii. 6. The Septuagint, in using this word in Gen. viii. 13, "removed the *covering* of the ark," perhaps means not the whole of the roof but the *covering of the trap-door or window in the roof*, through which Noah "looked."

meant (or if he did, that his original authority may not have meant) "roof," but "trap-door in the roof." It would be hazardous to dogmatise about the Ark; but the impression left by the passage above quoted is that Noah is not to be understood as unroofing the whole of the Ark when he looked out. And here we can hardly believe (whether Mark believed it or not) that the original Gospel described the paralytic's friends as unroofing the whole house.

[200] The rendering of the Revised Version "they uncovered the roof," is neither quite accurate nor literal. To "uncover" a thing is to take a cover from the whole of it. "Uncover the roof," would be appropriate here to signify the removal of a tarpaulin from the whole of the roof, but not, except loosely, the removal of the roof from the whole of the building, and certainly not the removal of a few tiles, nor the opening of a trap-door. Again, it is not literal, because it does not express the fact that the Greek repeats the same word in noun and verb. Fairly literal renderings would be "they *uncovered* the *cover*," "*unroofed* the *roof*," "took off the *covering* of the *cover*"; and the last of these would approach the meaning of the original, which probably meant, either "they lifted up the cover of the trap-door in the roof," or "they lifted up the trap-door that covered the roof-window." In the former case, we must suppose a trap-door protected by a shutter to keep out rain and dust; in the latter, simply a trap-door covering a hole used as a door.

[201] We learn from the *Horae Hebraicae*, in its comment on the present passage in Mark, that a lodger in the attic of a Jewish house was sometimes not allowed to use the interior house-stairs, but was compelled to go up the exterior staircase to the house-top and thence to descend into his room by the trap-door in the roof. This, no doubt, was to secure privacy for the family. But where the upper room was not let, it would seem that in many cases the roof

trap-door, with its awkward arrangement of a rope-ladder[1] for descent into the attic, would be disused. The door—or the cover, if there was one—would then be firmly fastened to be secure against rain, and possibly against robbers. Thus it might be wedged into the roof so fast that it would need considerable effort to force it out.

[202] And this might explain Mark's remarkable word, most inadequately translated by the Revised Version " broken up." No instance has been alleged from Greek literature to shew that the word could have this meaning ; it means " dig out," and is applied frequently to the " gouging out " of an eye from the socket. In its strict sense it would most aptly and graphically express the effort needed to extricate the trap-door or shutter from the grooves into which it was wedged.

[203] The hypothesis of a trap-door in the roof disposes at once of all the objections that have been brought by Strauss against the truth of Mark's narrative on the supposition that it commits those who accept it to a belief that the roof was " broken up," with the necessary consequence of tiles, plaster, and rubbish falling on the heads of those who were assembled round Jesus in the room below. The difficulty of such a supposition may well have induced Matthew to omit all Mark's details as being the result of a misunderstanding. It should be added that Luke's expression " through the tiles " does not commit him to the view that they were " broken up." " The tiles " often means in Greek, as well as in Latin, " the [tiled] roof." Perhaps Luke assumed the trap-door, but that must remain uncertain.[2]

---

[1] Wetstein on Mk. ii. 4 quotes Plutarch, *Cap. Rom.* v. p. 264 D τὴν ὑπὲρ τὸ τέγος εἰς τὴν οἰκίαν καθίμησιν. But the arrangement may have been different for Jewish houses.

[2] It is quite in Luke's manner to denote "roof" first by "house-top" when the question is of "mounting" to it, and then by "tiles" when the question is of descending, as Cicero says, "through the tiles," *i.e.* through the trap-door in the tiled roof. See note from Wetstein quoted below [208].

CONFUSIONS OF WORDS [205]

(*b*) " *The trap-door-in-the-roof :* "   *Why not expressly mentioned by Mark ?*

[204] It is a very obvious question to ask why Mark, instead of giving us a long and ambiguous account about a " roof-cover " or " cover," does not definitely mention the roof-trap-door. The answer is that the Hebrew word that means " roof-window," being rare and technical, might easily be misunderstood by him. It occurs nine times in the Bible, meaning " lattice," " sluice," " window." In the last signification it denotes a horizontal, not a vertical, window, and is five times translated by a rare Greek word that implies " crashing down," retained in the English " cataract." This is a very natural word to denote a " falling door," *i.e.* " trap-door." But the Hebrew is very similar to that of the much more common word " four." And further, since the same Hebrew preposition may mean " in," " at," or " by " (whether implying agency or neighbourhood), it follows that "*at the trap-door*" could easily be taken as meaning "*by four.*"

[205] This latter rendering Mark has adopted. But it was not unnatural that some dissatisfaction should be felt with it, partly because of the existence of other traditional explanations, partly because the omission of " men " in such a phrase appears to be unusual in Hebrew. Hence other marginal glosses would spring up. Now the Hebrew for " four " is said to be identical with the Aramaic for "stretcher." Hence later evangelists, while adopting the *letters* of Mark's alteration of the Hebrew text from " trap-door " to " four," might arrive at an entirely different meaning ; and thus we find Matthew and Luke, instead of " by *four,*" substituting " on *a bed.*"[1]

---

[1] " Roof-window," or " trap-door in the roof," used of " the windows of heaven," is rendered καταρράκτης, Gen. vii. 11, viii. 2, 2 K. vii. 19, Mal. iii. 10 ; " roof-window" = ארבה : " four " = ארבעה, which is said by Professor Marshall in the *Expositor* to mean " stretcher " in Aramaic. (Hebr. רבץ = Aram. רבע, but this = κοίτη rather than κλίνη.)

121

§ 14. *The healing of the paralytic: origin of Mark's details*

[206] It is possible that Matthew's omission of Mark's details is due to the fact that they were not a part of Mark's Hebrew or even Greek original, but the result of a Hebrew gloss, or marginal note, added by some early evangelist or editor attempting to explain a disputed passage. Wishing to express his view of the tradition about "letting down through the roof, or, through the tiles," this editor may have written, "They found not how they should bring him in because of the multitude, and they caused-to-go-up (*i.e.* lifted up) the roof-cover, and let the man down."

[207] When incorporating this note with details added to make the meaning clear, "Mark"—*i.e.* not Peter's nephew but the editor, or one of the editors, through whom Mark's Gospel has come down to us—may possibly have forgotten the difference between the lighter roofs in the West and the more solid ones used in the East for sleeping and walking in the cool of the evening. Strabo and other writers unquestionably use Mark's word (R.V., " uncover ") for " unroof," and mention cases of large buildings completely and rapidly unroofed with ease ; Strabo speaks of a temple unroofed in a single day. It is therefore possible that " Mark "—*i.e.* Mark's editor—may have believed that the roof was rapidly and completely unroofed by "digging out (the tiles)," and that this misunderstanding may explain his use of that particular verb. But we are not committed to "Mark's" belief. Our hypothesis is that he is in error, but that his erroneous tradition helps us to go back to the original truth.[1]

Matthew has rejected the whole as a conflation, or late tradition ; and this it is, but in the main a true one, or at all events leading to the truth.

[208] Luke took "caused-to-go-up" as "went up to,"

[1] On the probability that Mark passed through many editions, see the warning above, p. xv., n. ii., and 325*a*.

and the "roof-cover" as the "roof," or "house-top." In describing the paralytic as let down "through the tiled roof" —which is the regular meaning of "tiles" both in Latin and Greek—Luke may be steering a middle course. He mentions "tiles," but not "digging out." He does not mention—but he may imply—"the trap-door in the roof."[1]

[**209**] The view that Mark's addition results from a Hebrew gloss harmonises with the conjecture that Luke's "went up" corresponds to a causative ("caused to go up") in the original of Mark. There is also some slight positive evidence for it in the parallelism between (Mark) "not being *able*" and (Luke) "not *finding*." Compare a passage in Job where the Hebrew has "they *had found no* answer," but the Septuagint "they *were not able* to answer."[2]

If the hypothesis of "letting down through *the trap-door*" is correct, and if it was altered by Mark to "four" and by others to "bed," it is an error curiously similar to that above mentioned (**30**) wherein a scribe altered "let down by *a basket* (sportam)" into "let down by *the gate* (portam)"— alleged by Bacon as an instance of the tendency to alter the unknown into the known.

§ 15. (*Mark*) "*making a way*," (*Luke*) "*rubbing with their hands*"

There follow two instances of the mistranslation of a Hebrew word that means, as a noun, "way," and, as a verb, "make one's way," "tread a way (habitually)," "tread [grapes, olives, or corn]," "trample."

---

[1] A trap-door appears to be implied in Milton, *Par. L.* iv. 191, describing a thief, who "in at the window creeps or o'er *the tiles*." Comp. Cicero, *Philipp.* ii. 18 (Wetstein on Mk. ii. 4), contrasting "entrance across the threshold" with "letting down through *the tiles* (per tegulas demittere)."

[2] Job xxxii. 3, "had found (מצא)," ἠδυνήθησαν. This is not a mistranslation, but a free translation such as might be expected in Job and Mark.

(i.) Mark iv. 4	Matth. xiii. 4	Luke viii. 5
"Some fell by the side of the way, and *there came* the birds and devoured it."	"Some (pl.) fell by the side of the way, and, *having come*, the birds devoured them."	"Some fell by the side of the way, and *it was trampled down* and the birds of the heaven devoured it."

[210] The original was, nearly as Luke, "and they [*i.e.* people] trampled it down and the birds of the heaven devoured it." The Hebraic use of the impersonal "they" escaped Mark's notice, so that he made "the birds" the subject. Then, since birds do not "trample" the seed, he was forced to take the verb as meaning "made their way," or, more simply, "came," thus: "And there made their way to it the birds of the heaven and devoured it."[1]

(ii.) Mark ii. 23	Matth. xii. 1	Luke vi. 1
"And it came to pass, that he on the sabbath was going on through the cornfields, and his disciples began to *make a way*, plucking the ears."	"In that season went Jesus on the sabbath through the corn-fields: but his disciples were hungry and began to pluck ears and eat."	"But it came to pass on a sabbath that he was going on through corn-fields and his disciples were plucking the ears and eating, *rubbing* [them] *with their hands.*"

[211] Mark's expression "make *a way*," if it represented the historical fact, would have to be faced as Euthymius faced it, admitting that the disciples "tore up the wheat-ears that they might be able to go on."[2] Matthew and Luke

---

[1] [210*a*] The verb hardly ever means simply "come." Even when it is thus translated in Num. xxiv. 17, "There shall *come forth* a star out of Moab," ἀνατελεῖ, there seems to be a notion of making way through obstruction.

[2] [211*a*] Euthym. on Mt. xii. 1 (quoted by Field, *Otium N.* on Mk. ii. 23), ἀνέσπων τοὺς στάχυας ἵνα προβαίνειν ἔχοιεν. Kypke (on Mk. ii. 23) is unable to allege a single instance in which ὁδὸν ποιῶ ("I make *a road*") is used like ὁδὸν ποιοῦμαι ("I make *my way*"). Even the single instance which he takes as passive is really a middle (Liban. *Epist.* 718), ὑπὲρ ἀδελφοῦ τὴν ὁδὸν 'Τ. ἔφη ταυτηνὶ

omit the difficult phrase; and, by adding that the disciples "ate" (Matthew adds also "they were hungry"), they meet, by anticipation, the charge of wanton trespass implied in the scholarlike interpretation of Mark's words. The difficulty raised by them in early times may be estimated by the fact that the Arabic Diatessaron omits them, and the Sinaitic Syrian alters them into "and his disciples ate the ears."

[212] The explanation lies in Luke's expression, "rubbing them with their hands." In classifying their prohibitions of sabbath work, the Jews distinguished between "primitive" and "derivative" labour. To reap was "primitive," and was of course forbidden. But to pluck corn was a kind of reaping, *deriving* an unlawfulness from its analogy with reaping, and was consequently forbidden also. In the same way they forbade "derivative" ploughing and grinding, and declared that a man who on the sabbath rubbed wheat-ears on the palms of his hands, and then blew away the husk, and ate them, was "guilty."[1]

[213] Now the word "trample," above mentioned, though usually applied to the treading of olives or grapes, is at least once applied to the treading of corn, and is translated by the

πεποιῆσθαι. ἐφωράθη δὲ ὑπὲρ σοῦ μᾶλλον ἢ ὧν ἔφη πεποιημένος, "he said he had made . . . he was convicted of *having made*."

[211*b*] The best MSS read ὁδοποιεῖν in Mk. This, in the LXX always (5) means "prepare (or, make) a road." The inferior MSS read ὁδὸν ποιεῖν, which, unless ὁδόν is defined by a pronoun, must mean the same thing. The only passage quoted from the LXX to the contrary is Judg. xvii. 8, "as he journeyed," (Heb.) "in-making (לעשׂות) his way (דרכו)," τοῦ ποιῆσαι τὴν ὁδὸν αὐτοῦ. This proves that the LXX did not mind saying ποιεῖ ὁδὸν αὐτοῦ for ὁδὸν ποιεῖται; but it does not prove that the LXX, or any one else, ever used ὁδὸν ποιεῖ (without αὐτοῦ) to mean anything but "he makes a road." This, then, until some instance is alleged to the contrary, must be taken to be the meaning here.

[1] [212*a*] (Wetst. on Mt. xii. 2) *Beza*, f. xiii. 2: "Qui fricat spicas tritici, sufflat super manum et edit; si autem sufflavit et in sinum recondidit, reus est. R. Eleasar dixit: 'Et sic sabbato.'" Presumably the two actions were forbidden as being "derivative" threshing and winnowing, and therefore a breach of the sabbath.

125

Septuagint "thresh."[1] But a translator, not familiar with the subtleties of sabbatical "derivative" works, might naturally take the verb in its radical sense, that is to say, as being the causative of "way." It sometimes means "make a way for others," or "guide." But here there was no question of "guiding." He might therefore leave out "for others," and translate the perplexing word with honest literalism. This Mark appears to have done, leaving posterity to deal with the difficulty—"*make a way.*"

[214] But "trample" (drk) is not unlike "pound," or "beat" (dk'k'), which is specially applied to corn, and the latter is once rendered "trample," possibly being confused with the former.[2] And, again, the latter appears once—possibly being taken to mean "champ," "crush" in the teeth—to be rendered "eat."[3] Possibly Matthew followed a tradition substituting the latter for the former, and taking the meaning to be "champ," or "eat." At all events Matthew inserts "eat," and does not insert anything else corresponding to Mark's "made a way," or Luke's "rubbing them with their hands."

Luke explains the "treading" or "derivative threshing" in plain words as "rubbing with their hands." Perhaps, also, he too (like Matthew) adopted דקק, and interpreted it as "champ" or "eat," conflating the two interpretations.

[215] Many details in this attempt at restoration of the original are conjectural. The Hebrew may have had דקק, "crush," instead of a form of דרך, "way," and Mark may have corrupted the former into the latter. And there is a great deal to be said for this view, as "way" is far more common than "crush."

[216] Two conclusions, however, are certain, viz. (i.) that no scholar is at present justified in taking Mark to

---

[1] Jer. li. 33, "like a threshing-floor when *it is trodden*," ἀλοᾶν.
[2] Is. xxviii. 28, דקק (Tromm.), καταπατήσει; דרך = (4) καταπατεῖν.
[3] Is. xxviii. 27, דקק (Tromm.) βρωθήσεται (the LXX is greatly confused).

mean anything but what Euthymius took him to mean, and (ii.) that this meaning is historically impossible.

[217] Two others are highly probable, viz. that (i.) Luke is right, and (ii.) the difference between Luke and Mark (and Matthew) may be explained by original obscure Hebrew and by mistranslation from it. This last derives such increase of probability from the preceding instance in the Parable of the Sower that it may be regarded as almost certain.

[218] It is possible that the Original included a word translated by Luke "with their hands," but meaning literally "with the palms [of their hands]." This word means, etymologically, the bend or hollow of the hand, *or the foot*, and it is rendered twelve times by the Septuagint "footprint," but in all but two of these occasions the Hebrew "palm" is accompanied by "of the foot." The only instance in which "footprint" is used for "palm" by itself is in the description of the "cloud as small as a man's *hand*," where the Septuagint has "a man's footprint."[1] If this word was a part of the original, Mark mistook "threshing with the palms [of their hands]" for "trampling with the soles [of their feet]."

[1] 1 K. xviii. 44, ὡς ἴχνος ἀνδρός.

CHAPTER IV

CONFUSIONS OF IDIOM

§ 1. (*Mark*) "*Before the cock crow twice thrice* . . ."

[219] Mark, alone among the Synoptists, represents Jesus as predicting (not only the exact number of denials, but also) the number of times that the cock would crow before Peter thrice denied his Master :—

Mark xiv. 30	Matth. xxvi. 34	Luke xxii. 34
". . . thou . . . before the cock crow *twice*, shalt deny me thrice."	". . . before the cock crow, thou shalt deny me thrice."	". . . the cock shall not crow . . . until thou shalt thrice deny that thou knowest me."

The omission of "twice" by Matthew and Luke is all the more remarkable because its presence would seem to many to enhance the miraculousness of the prediction.

[220] The explanation is as follows : "Twice" may be expressed in Hebrew by "*times* two." But the Hebrew "time"—which also means "step," "stroke," "way," "course," etc.—is one of the few nouns that are occasionally used in the dual; and the dual of any noun, when without vowel-points, is indistinguishable from the plural. This ambiguity necessarily produces confusion sometimes where "two" is in question. For example, the Revised Version of Prov. xxviii. 6 gives in the text "perverse in [his] *ways*," but in

the margin, "lit. 'perverse of *two ways.*'"[1] So in Num. ix. 22, "whether it were *two-days,* or a month, or a year (lit. days)," the LXX has simply *"the days* of a month"; and even the MSS. that frequently correct the LXX, so as to make it conform to the Hebrew, drop the "two" here.[2] So in translating the dual of "time" in Eccles. vi. 6, "a thousand years *twice-told* (lit. *times-two*)," the LXX takes it as the plural of "course," and has *"the courses* of a thousand years." A still more important passage, and one exactly applicable to the passage from Mark under consideration, is:—

[221] Job xxxiii. 29 (R.V.): "Lo, all these things doth God work *twice* [*yea*] *thrice* [A.V. "oftentimes"] with a man." The Hebrew "twice thrice" appears to mean "repeatedly," being used like our "two or three times," only with a rather ampler meaning. But, whatever be its exact shade of meaning, it is easy to see that the omission of "or," "yea," or some similar particle, may sometimes cause ambiguity. Still further may a translator be perplexed if "twice," being represented by a Hebrew form that *may mean either "times-two" or "times,"* comes—as it does in the extract from Job—immediately before a word that regularly *does* mean "three"[3] but in this particular context *may* mean "thrice." How natural for a Greek, in such circumstances, to translate the Hebrew by "*times* (or, *courses, ways,* etc.) *three*"! Now this is precisely what the Septua-

---

[1] [220*a*] Comp. Prov. xxviii. 18, "he that is perverse *in* [*his*] *ways*" (marg. "walketh perversely *in* two ways"). In neither instance does the LXX express the "two." In Dan. viii. 3, 6, 20, describing a "ram with two horns," "two," being expressed by the dual, is omitted both by LXX and by Theodotion.

[2] [220*b*] Num. ix. 22, LXX μηνὸς ἡμέρας (AF ημερας η μηνος ημερας). The Hebrew representation of "a year" by "days" naturally perplexed the LXX. So in 1 S. i. 5, "one portion of *two-persons*"; LXX has simply "one portion." Judg. v. 30, "a damsel [nay] *two-damsels,*" is quite differently rendered both by LXX and by A.

[3] שלוש.

gint has done in Job: "Lo, all these things doth the Mighty One work *three ways* with a man."

[222] Now, applying these facts to the passage in Mark under discussion, we find all the discrepancies explicable by a Hebrew original of this kind :—

"Before the cock crow,[1] twice [or] thrice" [lit. "times-two [or] three," capable of being rendered "times-three"] "shalt thou deny me."

(i.) Mark translates this literally. But our present text so arranges the words as to necessitate the meaning "Before the cock crow twice, thrice shalt thou deny me."

(ii.) Matthew, like the Septuagint in Job, takes the meaning to be "times-three," and renders it by the Greek "thrice," thus : "Before the cock crow, *thrice* thou shalt deny me."

(iii.) In this new form, the meaning depends on punctuation. It might mean, "Before the cock crow thrice, thou shalt deny me." Luke, aware of conflicting traditions springing from Greek and Hebrew ambiguities, throws the prediction into a new form in which no ambiguity is possible : "The cock shall not crow till thrice thou shalt deny that thou knowest me."

§ 2. (*Mark and Matthew*) "*after two days,*" (*Luke*) "*drawing nigh*"

[223] The Hebrew of "after *two days*" has been shewn (220) to be indistinguishable (without vowel-points) from

---

[1] [222a] That is, "before *cock-crow*," a term recognised for early morning or late night. It is interesting to note that Mark alone, the traditional interpreter of St. Peter, mentions (Mk. xiii. 35) "cock-crow" as one of the critical seasons when the Master may "come."

If Mark, Peter's nephew, retained the Hebrew idiom "twice [or] thrice" by writing πρὶν ἀλέκτορα φωνῆσαι δὶς τρὶς . . . , it was natural that "or," *i.e.* ἤ, should be inserted in the margin by a very early editor. But subsequent editors would dislike the notion that Jesus should make, as it were, an *alternative* prediction ("twice, *or possibly* thrice"). Hence some might transfer the ἤ to a different place in the text, placing it after πρίν. Codex B has πρὶν ἤ here, but πρίν in Mk. xiv. 72. The text of Mk. xiv. 30 varies greatly.

that of "after *days.*" But the latter expression is frequently used in the Bible for "after *some days*," mostly meaning "after *many* days, or *several* days." Now suppose, in a context where it was clear that the interval was *not* one of many days, a Greek translator mistook "two days" for "days." Would he not naturally desire to make it clear that, in this particular instance, "days" meant "few days"? This is what Luke appears to have done (by using a paraphrase "drawing nigh") in the following passage:—

Mark xiv. 1	Matth. xxvi. 2	Luke xxii. 1
"Now there was the Passover and the [feast of] unleavened bread *after two days.*"	". . . *after two days* the Passover cometh."	"There was *drawing nigh* the feast of unleavened bread, called Passover."[1]

§ 3. (*Matthew*) "*two . . . for a farthing,*" (*Luke*) "*five . . . for two farthings*"

[224] The Hebrew "two three," for "two or three," is on one occasion translated by the Septuagint "two *and* three,"[2] and this, taken literally, might be replaced by an equivalent "five." But "two" by itself may mean "a few," in the Bible, as in the passage where the widow of Zarephath says, "I am gathering two sticks." Matthew himself evidently regards "two" as synonymous with "two or three," when he writes, "If *two* of you shall agree," and, a little afterwards, "for where *two or three* are gathered together in my name."[3] These facts explain:—

---

[1] [223*a*] Comp. Mk. ii. 1, "after days," δι' ἡμερῶν, with Lk. v. 17, ἐν μιᾷ τῶν ἡμερῶν. If the Hebrew for "after" is here "from" (מ-), used partitively, Luke may have taken it as meaning "one of." If the original was אחר, "after," it should be remembered that this is repeatedly confused with אחד, "one."

[2] Amos iv. 8.

[3] 1 K. xvii. 12, Mt. xviii. 19, 20. "A couple" is similarly used in many parts of England.

Matth. x. 29	Luke xii. 6
"Are not *two* sparrows sold for a farthing?"	"Are not *five* sparrows sold for *two* farthings?"

[225] The original was, "Are not *two* [*or*] *three* sparrows sold for a farthing?" Some interpreted this as "two *and* three" (as in Amos above). Hence arose an insertion of "five" in the margin. Similarly, we have found the LXX (**79**) conflating "the *tenth*, on the *first*" into "the *eleventh*."

Others, taking it (perhaps correctly) to mean "two or three" in the sense of "a few," nevertheless thought (as Matthew above) that the phrase might be conveniently abbreviated, and that the meaning was expressed by "two." Hence would arise various marginal annotations and confused traditions about "two" and "five," and, among these, Luke's tradition, applying "five" to "sparrows" and "two" to "farthings." But Matthew represents the spirit (though not the letter) of the original, taking the phrase to mean "a few," and condensing it, as he does elsewhere, into "two."[1]

---

[1] Two other explanations are given of this variation, both of them unsatisfactory.

(i.) "A proverb about cheapness might be current in two forms, (*a*) 'two for one farthing,' (*b*) 'five for two'; Christ, in His teaching, might sometimes use one, sometimes the other." This is open to the objection that the proverb is used here not as a detached saying—likely to be often repeated and varied—but as a part of a connected discourse (eight verses) which we have no reason to suppose to have been repeated, and which Matthew and Luke give in parallelism verse by verse.

(ii.) "In Luke's time the price of sparrows had risen, and he did not like to state what was untrue, so gave what he knew to be the market-price." But it would be both "untrue" and irreverent to represent Christ as saying what He did not say. Few historians, especially if they professed to know things "accurately," would alter, for example, "*a penny* a day," into "*three half-pence* a day," because of a rise in wages since the utterance of the former phrase—still less if the utterance proceeded from one whom they believed to be the Son of God.

§ 4. (*Mark*) "*after three days*," (*Matthew and Luke*) "*on the third day*"

[226] The perplexity of the Septuagint in rendering passages where "or" is omitted is illustrated by its rendering of the words of Jonathan to David: "About to-morrow [or] the third [day]." Here the Greek drops "to-morrow"—although there is no cause for confusion in the word—and gives "when-as the season threefold."[1] Much more easily might a Greek translator drop "two" when it is represented by the dual of the word "days," as in the following expression used by Hosea, "after two-days [lit. *days* (dual)] in day the third." Here "in" is represented by a single letter, easily dropped owing to its similarity with the letter that precedes it. But the dropping of it would leave the translator with a passage that he might very pardonably take as "after days day three," and render freely as "after three days." Moreover, "after" is often confused with "in," and (78) cardinal and ordinal numbers ("three" and "third") are interchangeable.[2] This probably explains the discrepancy in the predictions about Christ's resurrection:—

Mark viii. 31   Matth. xvi. 21   Luke ix. 22
". . . and *after*   ". . . and *on the*   ". . . and *on the*
three days rise again." *third day* be raised   *third day* be raised
                           up."   up."

[227] The departure of Matthew and Luke from Mark is probably not caused, or at all events not wholly caused, by a desire to bring the narrative into conformity with the current account of the interval between Christ's death and

---

[1] I S. xx. 12, "about the time of (כעת) to-morrow (מחר) [or] the third [day] (השלישית)," ὡς ἂν ὁ καιρὸς τρισσῶς.

[2] Hos. vi. 2, "After (-מ) two-days (ימים) in (-ב) day (יום) the-third (השלישי)." The LXX translates it correctly: ב, *i.e.* "in," has been noted above [158*a*] as often confused with ם (or מ), *i.e.* "after."

resurrection. It is highly probable that the original contained a modified quotation from the passage of Hosea above mentioned : " He will cause us to live after two-days in the third day he will raise us up "—substituting " him," or " the Son of Man," for " us." If the prediction was in this form and was erroneously rendered by Mark owing to his misunderstanding of the dual for the plural in the first half of the prophecy, it was very natural that later evangelists should avoid the first half as superfluous, and content themselves with the second.

§ 5. (*Matthew*) " *seventy times seven*," (*Luke*) " *seven. times turn* "

Matthew gives these words as part of a reply to Peter's question, " How often shall I forgive my brother ? " Luke's parallel occurs, not in a reply, but in the course of a general exhortation :—

Matth. xviii. 22

"Jesus saith unto him, I say not unto thee until seven times, *but* until *seventy times seven*."

Luke xvii. 4

" And if seven times in the day he sin against thee and *seven times turn* to thee saying, I repent, thou shalt forgive him."

[228] The original probably contained an allusion to the ancient law of revenge mentioned by Lamech, " If Cain shall be avenged seven-fold, truly Lamech *seventy-and-seven-fold*."[1] But Matthew follows the Septuagint, which substitutes 490 for 77. This mistake was sure to be attacked by Jewish opponents of the Church, and it was natural for Luke to take advantage of any possibility of so interpreting the Hebrew Gospel as to give a different rendering of the original.

[1] Gen. iv. 24, "seventy (שבעים) and seven-fold (שבעה)," but LXX ἑβδομηκοντάκις ἑπτά, *i.e.* "seventy times seven"—an error.

Supposing the original to have been "(a) but (b) seventy (c) and seven-fold," we will now show how Luke's version may have arisen by corruption and slight modification.

[229] (a) The Hebrew for "but," in this sense, is frequently "but *if*." This agrees with Luke's interpretation, "And *if*" (the difference between "and" and "but,"[1] in translating from Hebrew, being mostly a matter of taste).

[230] (b) The Hebrew for "seventy" is the Hebrew for "seven," *plus* the plural termination (*im*). "Seven" is sometimes used adverbially to mean "seven times." Also the plural termination (*im*) might easily be confused with *ivm*, "day"; thus "seventy" might become "seven times in the day."[2]

[231] (c) "And seven-fold" is very easily confused with "he shall turn," which in the Bible is frequently used for "turning (in repentance)."[3]

[232] The result of (a), (b), and (c) would be, "And if seven times in the day he shall turn." But if an evangelist conflated the old "seven-fold, or times" with the new "he shall turn," this would give: "And if seven times in the day and seven times he shall turn." This then might become current as an obscure tradition—requiring emendation—of what Jesus said as to the number of times that a disciple was to forgive his brother conditionally on repentance. Suppose Luke desired to insert this in the discourse that says (xvii. 3), "If thy brother sin, rebuke

[1] "But (כי) if (אם)" is given by Delitzsch here as the translation of Mt. "but (ἀλλά)."

[2] "Day (יום)" is often confused with "water (מים)," "in the day" once with the pl. of "son (בן)," "our days" once with "right hand (ימין)"—all of them less easy changes than that supposed above, viz. יום to יום.

[3] [231a] "He shall turn" = ישב, "and seven-fold" = שבעה. The difference is great at the first glance. But (i.) the gutturals are freely handled in Hebrew; (ii.) the two last letters might be taken by Luke as parts of "to thee," עליך; (iii.) when an editor finds the first and largest part of an obscure and disputed passage capable of being easily altered to an edifying result, it is very natural that he should feel justified in dealing more arbitrarily with the last part.

him; and if he repent, forgive him." It would only be necessary to supply something, in the obscure tradition, after "if," thus, "And if [*it should happen, or, he shall sin*] seven times in the day, and seven times he shall turn." When using the vaguer verb "turn" in place of the preceding "repent," Luke might naturally amplify "turn" for clearness, by adding, "saying, I repent." Then it would only remain to repeat the precept to forgive. The result would be, "And if he sin against thee seven times in the day, and seven times turn to thee, saying, I repent, thou shalt forgive him."[1]

§ 6. *On the error that led Luke to suppose that there were "other seventy [two] disciples"*

[233] It could be shown by a detailed examination that Luke's Seventy-Mission—as we will call it for brevity —contains nothing except variations and conflations of traditions given by Mark and Matthew in the Twelve-Mission. Without asking the reader to accept this statement till it is proved (which must be reserved for another treatise), we may just mention that the "sandals" and "money-belt" mentioned by Mark are omitted in Luke's Twelve-Mission, but appear in Luke's Seventy-Mission in the shape of "shoes" and "pouch." This ought to prepare the reader to give a patient hearing to a demonstration that "seventy [two]" may be explained as an error of Luke made in translating Mark's Hebrew original in the following :—

Mark vi. 7 (*The Twelve*) Luke x. 1 (*The Seventy*)
"And he (lit.) calleth to "But after these things the
him the Twelve and began Lord appointed other seventy

---

[1] [232*a*] Luke's acceptance of this form of the tradition would be facilitated by the fact that Jesus certainly implied "repentance" as a condition for the acceptance of forgiveness by the offender, if not for its pronouncement by the forgiver. *Hor. Hebr.* on Mt. xviii. 21 alleges Jewish traditions mentioning the "imploring" of the offender, and limiting the forgivenesses to three.

to send them (lit.) two two [W. H. add in brackets " two "] and sent them (lit.) by two [W. H. add in brackets " two "] . . . ."

[234] The omission of Mark's "two two," in Matthew's and Luke's Twelve-Mission, suggests that there was some obscurity in the Hebrew. This might well be. For "twelve" is in Hebrew "two ten," so that the substance of the Hebrew original of " He sent *twelve*, (lit.) *two two* " might be, " He sent *two ten two two.*" Now " twice " is rendered " two " by the Septuagint in the Psalms[1] ("*twice* have I heard the same"), and the verb "double" is repeatedly used in the sense of doing a thing a second time. Again, some forms of "two" resemble forms of a verb meaning "appoint," and the resemblance produces confusion once in Isaiah.[2] It is therefore possible that " two . . . two " might be corrupted into " He appointed . . . a second time." Lastly, the dual of the Hebrew " ten " (which closely resembles the singular) is so far similar to the Hebrew for " seventy " that the two are twice confused by the Septuagint.[3]

[235] Now " seventy " was recognised by the Jews as the number of the nations, or languages, of the earth,[4] so that it might seem highly appropriate for the appointment of a second group of disciples, perhaps regarded as typical of a future preaching of the Gospel to " the nations," *i.e.* the Gentiles. Thus prejudice and similarity of letters would combine to corrupt " ten " to " seventy," which would be placed in the margin. The result of these confusions would

---

[1] [234a] Ps. lxii. 12, δύο ταῦτα (78).

[2] Is. xi. 11, "the second time (שנית)," δείξει (leg. שנה). Comp. Lk. "appointed" ἀνέδειξεν.

[3] Gen. xi. 24, Ezra viii. 11, " twenty [lit. tens (dual)] (עשרים)," ἑβδομήκοντα (leg. שבעים). In Gen. xi. 17, (see context, Hebr. "four hundred and thirty," Gk. " three hundred and seventy") the LXX possibly takes "four (ארבע)" as "seven (שבע)." In 1 S. ix. 22, " about thirty (שלשים)," LXX has ἑβδομήκοντα.

[4] See Wetst. on Acts ii. 3.

be to produce a new tradition : " A second time he appointed (or, he repeated to appoint) seventy-two." The retention of "two" so as to make "seventy-two," instead of the more appropriate "seventy," is an indication of the stages through which the text has passed and of the honesty of those scribes who have not cancelled "two," in spite of its inconvenience.

[236] Finally Luke has conflated this with the statement that the Apostles were sent (lit.) "by two [two]." The reader may compare a somewhat similar conflation quoted above (77) from Daniel where " sixty-two weeks " is converted by the Septuagint into "seven and seventy and sixty-two."

§ 7. *Errors arising from the Hebrew "and"*

[237] The same Hebrew letter represents (i.) "and," (ii.) "even," meaning, "that is to say." Scores of consequent errors might be quoted from the Septuagint. Most important are those in which the Authorised differs from the Revised Version, or the Revised itself leaves the meaning an open question :—

1 Chr. xxi. 12 : " The sword of the Lord, *even* (marg. *and*) pestilence."

Judg. vii. 24 : "The waters as far as Bethbarah, *even* (R.V. marg. *and also*, A.V. *and*) Jordan."

Mal. iii. 1 : " The Lord . . . shall come . . . *and* (marg. and A.V. *even*) the messenger of the covenant."

In (R.V.) 1 K. vii. 45, parallel to 2 Chr. iv. 16, enumerating Temple-utensils, the former has "and the shovels, and the basins, *even* all these vessels"; the latter "and the shovels, and the flesh-hooks, *and* all the vessels thereof" —though the Hebrew conjunction is the same in both.

Ezra vi. 21 has "The children of Israel . . . *and* all such as had separated." But the "and" is omitted by the parallel 1 Esdr. vii. 13, presumably being taken by LXX to mean "even." The R.V. of 1 Esdr. vii. 13 inserts "even."

Nehem. viii. 7: "A., J., H., P., *and the* Levites" is parallel (with slight name-variations) to 1 Esdr. ix. 48, "A., K., A., Ph., *the* Levites."

Judg. vi. 25: "Thy father's bullock, *even* (marg. *and*) the second bullock." The Septuagint here has "and," but the MS that generally conforms the Septuagint to the Hebrew (Codex A) omits "and."

Zech. ix. 9: "... riding upon an ass, *even* upon a colt the foal (lit. son) of an ass (lit. she-ass)." So the Revised Version, but the Authorised and the Septuagint have "and."[1] This prepares us for:—

Mark xi. 2	Matth. xxi. 2	Luke xix. 30
"... a colt tied whereon no man hath yet sat."	"... *an ass* tied *and* a colt with her."	"... a colt tied whereon no man hath ever yet sat."

[238] Mark, followed by Luke, takes Zechariah's prophecy to refer to a single animal, and that not a "she-ass"—a creature of great value (superior to a "beast of burden") reserved for kings, nobles, judges, and prophets—but a mere colt. Interpreting "foal of a she-ass" to mean "not yet separated from its mother," Mark paraphrases it freely as "not yet used," *i.e.* whereon "no man hath yet sat."

[239] Matthew follows the Septuagint in taking the words to mean two animals. But in translating the prophecy in full, he mistranslates "Raise a shout, O daughter of Zion" as "Tell ye the daughter of Zion," differing from the Septuagint as well as from the Hebrew. He also calls the colt "the foal of a *beast of burden*," not "of a *she-ass*," missing the difference intended in the prophecy.

§ 8. *Indicative confused with non-indicative forms*

[240] (i.) Hebrew has no subjunctive. The future, "he will come," is identical with "he would come." (ii.) When

---

[1] The LXX renders "ass" by ὑποζύγιον, *i.e.* "beast of burden," and paraphrases "son of a she-ass" by πῶλον νέον, "young foal."

the future, "he will come," is preceded by "and," with a special vowel-point, it assumes the meaning of "and he *came*." (iii.) Hence, "The Lord spake unto him *that he should come*" is liable to be confused with "The Lord spake unto him *and he came*." Hence arises a general confusion between command and statement of fact.

2 Chr. xxxv. 3: "And he said to the Levites . . . *Put the holy ark* . . ." is rendered by the Septuagint "And *they put*"; but the parallel 1 Esdr. i. 3 has "And he spake unto the Levites . . . *by putting*."

[241] In the following instance two parallel *Hebrew* passages differ.

(i.) 2 K. xx. 7: "And Isaiah said, Take a cake of figs. And they took and laid it on the boil and he recovered."

(ii.) Is. xxxviii. 21: "And Isaiah [had] said,[1] Let them take a cake of figs and lay it for a plaster upon the boil and he shall recover."

(i.) LXX of Kings: "And he said, Let them take a cake of figs [the Codex Alexandrinus adds, "and it was taken"], and let them lay it on the sore, and he shall recover."[2]

(ii.) LXX of Isaiah: "And Isaiah said to Hezekiah, Take a cake of figs, and pound it and put it in a plaster and thou shalt be whole."

[242] Compare also (i.) Ezra v. 15: "He said unto him, *Take* these vessels," where LXX agrees, but (ii.) the parallel 1 Esdr. vi. 18 has (LXX) "And orders were given

---

[1] [241*a*] There is no pluperfect *tense* in Hebrew. The same word that means "said" in 2 K. must be rendered "*had* said" in Is. xxxviii., because the context and position of the clause demand it. But the pluperfect *meaning* is often required in an appendix or parenthesis, and the LXX seldom uses the Greek pluperfect to express it.

[2] The Hebr. ינקח="take." "*They took*"=ויקחו: נק occurs in two cases for "he took" instead of לקח.

The Hebr. ויחי may mean either "and he *recovered*" (as in K.), or "and he *shall recover*" (as in Isaiah).

unto him, *and he took* all these vessels . . . ," where R.V. has "that he should carry away."

Josh. ix. 21 : "And the princes said unto them, *Let them live.* So *they became* hewers of wood . . ."; LXX, "*They shall live,* and *they shall be* hewers of wood."

Josh. xxii. 8 : "He blessed them and spake unto them saying, *Return* with much wealth . . ."; LXX, "And he blessed them *and they departed* with much wealth."

Jer. xxxvii. 17 : "And the king asked him secretly in his house *and said* "; LXX, " And the king asked him secretly *to say.*" [1]

[243] The last passage may account for the astonishing fact that *Mark's account of the Mission of the Twelve contains no precept to preach the Gospel, or the Kingdom,* whereas such precepts are mentioned by Matthew and by Luke in the Mission of the Seventy as well as in that of the Twelve. For, according to the rule deducible from the preceding instances, an imperative may be latent in the following :—

Mark vi. 11-12

". . . Shake off the dust . . . for a testimony to them. And *having gone forth they preached . . .*"

We have only to suppose that the original was, " And *go forth and preach,*" and we then have a parallel to Matthew x. 7, "And as ye go, *preach,*" and Luke ix. 2, " He sent them *to preach* . . ."

Compare also :—

Mark xiv. 23	Matth. xxvi. 27
"*And they all drank* of it."	"*Drink ye all* of this."

---

[1] [242*a*] Comp. 1 K. xix. 11 : "And he said, Go forth and stand . . . And behold, the Lord *passed by* "; LXX, "And he said, Go forth . . . Behold the Lord *shall pass by.*" This is an example, not of the uncertainty of the meaning of ו, but of the uncertainty of the meaning of the Hebr. pres. participle. It shows how statement of fact may be confused with prediction.

§ 9. (*Mark*) "*they receive him*," (*Matthew and Luke*) "*he went*"

Mark iv. 36	Matth. viii. 23	Luke viii. 22
"And . . . *they receive him* . . . in the boat . . ."	"And, when he *went into* a boat . . ."	"And he himself went into a boat . . ." [Codex D, "went up," Ss. "went up and sat in a ship."]

[244] "*Receive.*"—Mark, in effect, has the causative "*cause-him-to-come* into the boat"; Matthew and Luke the non-causative "he *came* into the boat." This confusion of causative and non-causative is a constant cause of mistranslation in the Septuagint. Compare the following parallel passages in Kings and Chronicles, where the Hebrew text has the very word probably used by the original Hebrew Gospel here, namely, "go up" (which also means "go on board"), employed by Chronicles causatively and by Kings non-causatively. In Chronicles, the Septuagint mistranslates :—

1 K. x. 29	2 Chr. i. 17
"And a chariot *came up* and went out of Egypt"; LXX, lit. "there *came up* the going out."	"And they *fetched up* (lit. *caused to come up*) and brought out of Egypt a chariot"; LXX, "they *came in*" (Codex A, "they *came up*").

The reader will note that in Chronicles the later MS. (A) conforms to the Hebrew "up," whereas the earlier MSS. have "in." The difference of the Greek words there is precisely that between Codex D and most New Testament MSS. here.[1] Thus we see the phenomena of the Greek

[1] 2 Chr. i. 17 (see context of Chr. and K.) "And they fetched up (ויעלו)," ἐνέβαινον, A ἀνέβαινον. So in Lk. viii. 22 ἐγένετο . . . καὶ αὐτὸς ἐνέβη (Codex L ἀνέβη, D ἀναβῆναι αὐτόν).

Old Testament reproduced in this passage of the Greek New Testament—leading to the conclusion that the latter, like the former, is a translation.

§ 10. *Mark alone mentions "other boats"*

Matthew and Luke omit mention of the boats, as follows:—

Mark iv. 36	Matth. viii. 23.	Luke viii. 22.
". . . And other boats were with him."	". . . There followed him his disciples."	". . . And his disciples."

(i.) "*And other boats.*"

As Mark has just mentioned "the boat," he may have felt justified in supplying the noun here after "other," even though the original was only "and other[s] [were] with him."

[245] Now "other" is the same in Hebrew as "after," "behind," "backwards"; and the word "follow" is expressed in Hebrew by "be after" or "go after"; and "disciples," or "followers," might be expressed by a phrase with the same word. For instances of confusions based on this similarity see Prov. xxv. 9, "the secret of *another*," LXX "*backwards*"; Ps. xvi. 4, "*another*," LXX "*after* these things"; Sir. xlix. 5, "*backwards*," LXX "to *others.*" Possibly, in the Greek, "the *other*" may be intended to mean "the *next*," in Deut. xxix. 22, "the generation [*that is to come*] *afterwards,*" LXX "*the other* generation"; Gen. xvii. 21, "in the *next* year," LXX "*the other* year." Sometimes, too, confusion may have been caused by the fact that the same Greek preposition means "with" or "after," according to the case of the noun. In Exod. xxiii. 2, "thou shalt not *follow* a multitude," LXX has "thou shalt not *be with* a multitude"; and in 1 S. xiv. 13, "*after* him," LXX has "*with* him."[1]

[246] (ii.) "*With him.*"

---

[1] The word אחר ("after" and also "other") is used in all these passages; μετά with genit. means "with," with accus. "after" (**193a**).

Again the Hebrew "with-him," is, in one of its forms,[1] identical with "his-people," which may be used for "his attendants." In a parallel passage of Kings and Chronicles, "with him" and "the people" are interchanged, and the Septuagint omits "with him."[2] In Deut. xxxii. 43, apparently, and certainly in Josh. viii. 14, and in some MSS of Deut. iii. 1, "his people" is duplicated by the addition of "with him." The instances are numerous in which "people" and "with" are confused in the Septuagint.[3]

[247] Thus, taking (i.) "other" as "following," and (ii.) "with him" as "his disciples," Matthew might deduce "his *disciples followed* him," while Luke might consider "his people that followed him" to be sufficiently represented by "his disciples."

[248] There is probably a similar confusion between "disciples" and "follow" in Mt. viii. 21, "But another of *the disciples* said to him," which is parallel to Lk. ix. 59, "But he said unto another, *Follow me*" (where Matthew probably conflates). But the discussion of these passages must be deferred.

§ 11. (*Matthew*) "*destroying*," (*Luke*) "*casting*"

Matth. x. 28	Luke xii. 5
"But fear rather him who is able to *destroy* both soul and body in hell."	"Fear him who, after killing, hath authority to *cast* into hell."

[249] The context indicates free translation in one at least of the translators. But the following passages show that the divergence of "destroy" and "cast," *i.e.* "cause to go," may be explained by Hebrew corruption :—

---

[1] עמו.

[2] 1 K. viii. 62: "And all Israel *with him* (עמו)" = 2 Chr. vii. 4, "And all *the people* (עם)." The LXX of K. om. "with him" (but A inserts it).

[3] Dan. ix. 26, "*people*," LXX μετά, Theod. σύν; 1 Chr. xii. 18, "*with* thee," LXX "thy *people*," Ps. xlvii. 9, cx. 3, "*people*," μετά, etc.

CONFUSIONS OF IDIOM [251]

Lev. xxvi. 41 : " I *brought* them *into* the land " ; LXX, " I will *destroy* them *in* the land.
Dan. ii. 12 : " to destroy," Theod. as Hebr., but LXX " to *lead* out."[1]

Probably the original was " cause to go in(to) hell," and Matthew, interpreting it as " destroy in hell," added " soul and body," to signify that the Greek word, which sometimes means " lose," or " ruin," meant here utter destruction.

§ 12. (*Matthew*) "*fall to the ground without*," (*Luke*) "*forgotten in the sight of*"

[250] A word may be correctly translated, but in two different senses. For example, the word " fall " may mean " fall to the ground " (i.) metaphorically, *i.e.* be forgotten, despised, or (ii.) literally, *i.e.* perish. And this appears partly to explain :—

Matth. x. 29
"And one of them [*i.e.* the sparrows] shall not *fall to the ground without* your Father."

Luke xii. 6
" And one of them is not *forgotten in the sight of* God."

(i.) (*Matthew*) "*fall*," (*Luke*) "*forgotten*."

[251] (i.) The Hebrew " fall " is used metaphorically concerning (*a*) the words of Samuel which God did not allow to be unfulfilled, (*b*) days that are to be " void," and (*c*) a person of inferior account.[2] But these metaphorical

---

[1] Lev. xxvi. 41, והבאתי (from בוא), ἀπολῶ; Dan. ii. 12, להוברה, Theod. ἀπολέσαι, LXX ἐξαγαγεῖν (which=הביא in Ezek. xvii. 12) ; האביד (hiph.)= " destroy," הביא=" cause to go." Luke's word " cast (ἐμβάλλειν) " is used in a mistranslation of בוא in Hag. ii. 16. Matthew's "rather" (not a Hebraic word) suggests that he is translating freely.

[2] 1 S. iii. 20 ; Num. vi. 12, " the days . . . shall be *void* (A.V. *lost*)," ἄλογοι ; Job xiii. 2, " *inferior* to you," lit. " *fallen*," ἀσυνετώτερος.

Mr. W. S. Aldis suggests to me that there may have been a confusion between (*a*) שכח (" forget ") and (*b*) כשל (" fall "). In that case (*a*) would be the original, because (*b*) mostly means " stagger," " totter," and could not be applied to birds.

See also Sir. xliv. 10, " come to an end (שבת)," ἐπιλανθάνεσθαι, Sir. xlvii. 22, " he will suffer to fall to the ground (יפיל ארצה)," διαφθαρῇ (א[c.a.] διαφθείρῃ).

senses are comparatively rare. Perhaps no exact parallel could be quoted to Luke's use of the word, on the hypothesis that he translated the Hebrew "fall."

(ii.) (*Matthew*) "*without*," (*Luke*) "*in the sight of*"

[252] In Greek, Matthew's phrase "*not without*," when preceding "God," "divine fortune," etc., generally refers to *good* fortune, or what is sometimes called "a providential dispensation." But in Hebrew the phrase has not necessarily this good association, as appears from a Jewish tradition how a Rabbi and his son, in hiding during the days of persecution, sat at the door of their cave and watched a fowler catching birds. To them the fowler signified the heathen, and the birds the souls or lives of the persecuted. A Voice from heaven cried "Save thyself, save thyself" (or, as some say, "Pity, pity"). Then the bird escaped. At other times the Voice was against the bird and then it was caught. "Even a bird," exclaimed the Rabbi, "*without heaven* is not caught: how much less the soul of man!"[1]

Matthew's tradition, verbally accurate, but liable to misinterpretation, might induce Luke to adopt any variation (springing from a corruption of the original Hebrew) that might give an unambiguous and edifying meaning.

[253] The original of Matthew's "without" was probably "*away-from* the eyes of," *i.e.* without the knowledge of. But this form occurs only four times to a hundred occurrences of "*in* the eyes of." The latter, which would be the natural original of Luke's "in the sight of," differs from the former

---

[1] Schöttg. on Mt. x. 29. Wetst. gives the story with slight but interesting differences. The English reader must note that this saying takes the *bird's* point of view. The *fowler*—and perhaps a good many modern readers—might interpret it as meaning, "I cannot catch even a single bird without the help of heaven." But the meaning is, "The death even of a single bird is foreseen and controlled by God"; and the inference is that, though it may seem evil, there must be a good purpose underlying it.

[252*a*] "Without heaven" may throw light on Mt. "your father"=Lk. "God," the original being "heaven," variously paraphrased by Matthew and Luke.

by nothing but the difference of ם and ב—letters readily confused (158a). It is probable that the rarer form (Matthew's) was the original one, and that the authority followed by Luke altered it to the more usual form in order to harmonise with his interpretation of " fall."

§ 13. (*Matthew*) "*salute*," (*Luke*) "*do good to*"

[254] This variation occurs in the Sermon on the Mount, where Jesus, having inculcated "loving," proceeds to inculcate the expression of love in beneficent action. Deuteronomy *forbade* Israel to do good to, or "seek the peace" of, Ammonites and Moabites, but excepted the Edomite from this prohibition, " for he is thy brother." Jesus abrogated this rule, asking what virtue there was in mere "seeking the peace" of one's "brothers," who "do good to you" or "seek your peace." That this Deuteronomic precept permeated Jewish thought in the time of the composition of Ezra is proved by its quotation in that book.[1]

[255] But unfortunately the Hebrew "*seek* the peace of" is easily confused in translation with another quite distinct phrase, "*ask* [*after*] the peace of"; for the Hebrew "seek" is sometimes rendered by the Greek "ask," and the Hebrew "ask," though rarely, by the Greek "seek."[2] Now, "seek the peace of" is, in effect, "do good to." But "ask [after] the peace of" is simply "salute."

[256] Every one will recognise that these could easily be confused, and as a fact they are confused by the Septuagint, which, in the translation of the Deuteronomic precept itself —instead of "seek the peace"—gives, "Thou shalt not *accost them in words of friendship* and advantage to them."

[1] Deut. xxiii. 6, "Thou shalt not *seek* (דרש) their peace nor their prosperity all thy days for ever." Comp. Ezra ix. 10-12, "We have forsaken thy commandments which *thou hast commanded* . . . saying . . . The land . . . is an unclean land . . . neither take their daughters unto your sons, nor *seek* (דרש) their peace or their prosperity for ever."

[2] "Seek (דרש)" = (12) ἐπερωτᾶν; "ask (שאל)" = (2) ζητεῖν (Tromm.).

And it is significant that whereas in Ezra the Septuagint translates literally and correctly ("ye shall not *seek their peace*"), the parallel in Esdras is, "Ye shall not seek to *be at peace* with them." This, though not so serious an error as the one in Deuteronomy, does not express the Hebrew meaning "consult the interests of," "do good to."

[257] Matthew, though he reproduces Hebraic traditions and Hebraic thought perhaps more than any of the Synoptists, exhibits many instances of mistranslation from Hebrew, as we have seen in "the ass *and* the colt," and his use of the word "companion." We cannot therefore be surprised that he here falls into the error of the Deuteronomic Septuagint.

Matth. v. 47	Luke vi. 33
"And if ye *salute* your brethren [1] alone, what do ye more [than others]?"	"For if ye *do-good-to* them that do good to you, what thank have ye?"

[258] It may be noted that the Arabic Diatessaron renders Matthew thus: "If ye inquire for the good of your brethren only." The original was probably a play on words: "If ye seek *the peace of* (*shlm*) the men-of *your-peace* (*shlm*), what *recompense* (*shlm*) have ye?"[2] If so, Matthew has paraphrased as well as mistranslated, and Luke is substantially right.

§ 14. "*Man, thy sins are forgiven thee*"

Mark ii. 5	Matth. ix. 2	Luke v. 20
"And Jesus seeing their faith saith unto the paralytic, *Son*, thy sins are forgiven."	"And Jesus seeing their faith said unto the paralytic, *Be of good cheer, Son*, thy sins are forgiven."	"And seeing their faith he said, *Man*, thy sins are forgiven thee."

[1] Codex L has "friends."

[2] "Men of your peace" = "well-disposed," "friendly," rendered "friends" in Jer. xx. 10. It is mistranslated "recompense (ἀνταποδιδοῦσιν)" in Ps. vii. 4, and "having-received-recompense (ἀπεσχηκώς)" by Q marg. in Is. xlii. 19, where LXX omits it.

[259] "Man," when used in the Bible vocatively, implies reproach,[1] and is difficult to reconcile with "Son." Jesus never calls any man "son" except as the son of the Father in heaven;[2] but Luke would hardly have deviated so completely from Mark without some reason afforded by the text.

[260] Luke omits here "unto the paralytic"; and the question arises whether under that phrase there may be latent some explanation of the discrepancy. The original may not have repeated the technical term "paralytic" used at the introduction of the story, but may have called him "the sick (or, afflicted) man." Now this in Hebrew might be "*son-of affliction*."[3] This would explain how "son" made its way into the story.

[261] The next step is to ask whether "afflicted" could be confused with "man." That is answered by a passage where the Revised Version gives in its text "woeful," but in its margin an alternative "man," and by three passages where the Septuagint has "man" for "woeful." Suppose, then, that the original was "son of affliction," whether in the vocative, or in the objective after "said unto." Mark may have loosely conflated it first as "the paralytic" and then as "son." Luke, reading "son of affliction" as "son of man," took it vocatively as a term of reproach (which it is sometimes), and therefore equivalent to the Greek vocative "man."[4]

---

[1] Mic. vi. 8, Lk. xii. 14, xxii. 60, Rom. ii. 1, ix. 20. In Mic. vi. 8, the prophet appears to imply rebuke to Balak for even asking, "Shall I give my firstborn for my transgression?" In classical Greek ἄνθρωπε means "fellow."

[2] The Greek is τέκνον, "child." The pl. is used by Jesus to the disciples in Mk. x. 24, and the diminutive pl. (τεκνία) in Jn. xiii. 33—in both of which there is a special tenderness.

[3] Comp. Prov. xxxi. 5, "any that is afflicted"; Hebr. "all *the-sons-of affliction* (עני)," ἀσθενεῖς. This differs from the Hebr. for "affliction" supposed below. But the passage illustrates the Hebrew idiom.

[4] [261*a*] Jer. xvii. 16, "the *woeful* (אנוש) day" (marg. "some ancient versions read, *the judgment day of man*"). The word אנוש means "man," more especially in poetry, *e.g*. Ps. cxliv. 3, "son of man." The LXX have "man" in Jer. xvii. 9, 16, and Is. xvii. 11.

[262] But if this Hebrew word—meaning "afflicted" or "incurably diseased," but resembling "man"—was in the original, it opens up possibilities of explaining also Matthew's "be-of-good-cheer," a Greek word hardly ever used by the Septuagint except to express the Hebrew prohibition "do not fear." But this would not make very good sense here, where the context rather demands "Be hopeful, or trustful." Now the Hebrew "afflict" is confused once with "lift up," and "lift up" is used to mean "rejoice."[1] Hence, "son of affliction" might be interpreted by Matthew as "Son, *rejoice* (or, *be of good cheer*)."[2]

[263] There is a fair probability that the Synoptical divergence is due to this particular word in the original.[3] There is a very much stronger probability that it is due to *some* mistranslation from Hebrew. And it is certain that "man" is a mistake of Luke's.

§ 15. (*Mark*) "*nothing . . . except a staff*," (*Matthew*) "*nor a staff*," (*Luke*) "*neither a staff*"

These words occur in Christ's precepts to the Twelve, when He sent them forth to preach :—

Mark vi. 8	Matth. x. 9-10	Luke ix. 3
". . . that they should take nothing for [their] journey *except a staff alone*, no bread, no wallet . . ."	"Do not obtain gold . . . not a wallet for [your] journey . . . *nor* a staff."	"Take nothing for the journey, *neither* a staff, nor wallet, nor bread . . ."

[1] Jer. xxx. 12, "incurable (אנוש)," ἀνέστησα, leg. נשא; which (Is. xlii. 11) = εὐφράνθητι.

[2] [262a] The possibilities of error are increased by the fact that "forgive" may be in Hebrew "lift up," "bear," "take away"—the same word (נשא) that is confused with "afflicted (אנוש)" in Jer. xxx. 12. The juxtaposition of the two words might easily cause confusion, especially if the Hebrew verb was reduplicated.

[3] [263a] The exact meaning of אנש is "sick unto death." It occurs nine times in the Bible, and is only once (2 S. xii. 15, ἠρρώστησεν) rendered exactly. Elsewhere it = κατακρατεῖν (1), στέρεος (1), βίαιος (3), ἀνέστησα (1), ἄνθρωπος (2).

Beside the apparent contradiction as to the "staff," we have to explain why Matthew omits all mention of bread.

[**264**] The *Didaché*, or *Teaching of the Twelve Apostles*, says concerning the true apostle or missionary, "When he goeth forth let the missionary receive nothing except bread [to suffice him] until he reach his lodging for the night. But if he ask for money, he is a false prophet."[1] Now a sufficiency of bread is regarded in Hebrew as bread enough to *support* one, and hence is metaphorically called "the staff of bread";[2] and the writer appears to have read Christ's precept thus, "that they should take nothing for their journey *except the staff of bread*," i.e. bread enough to support them for the day, or, in other words, the "daily bread." This was almost certainly the original precept, but, if so, we may pronounce with equal certainty that it was intended in a spiritual sense. The Apostles were to go forth with nothing but the "daily bread" provided by the Father in heaven.[3]

The *Didaché*, though it has despiritualised, has at all events preserved, in a modified form, the old tradition, "nothing except the staff of bread." We have now to trace its developments in our Gospels.

[**265**] (i.) Mark, taking "staff" literally, was bound to detach it from "bread." But "nothing except a staff, bread, no wallet" would make no sense, and a very obvious way of making sense was to supply "no" as Mark does: "*no* bread, no wallet."[4]

[**266**] (ii.) Another development was to assume that

---

[1] *Didaché*, § xi. 6.

[2] Comp. Lev. xxvi. 26, Ps. cv. 16, Ezek. iv. 16, v. 16, xiv. 13.

[3] [**264***a*] It will be shewn hereafter that all the precepts in Mk. vi. 8-9 had originally a spiritual meaning. It is probable that Jesus laid down no rules at all about the literal food or clothing of the Apostles.

[4] [**265***a*] Mark (or his authority) might feel justified in this by the frequent omission of the Hebrew negative in *expression* when it has to be *implied* from a previous negative, *e.g.* (Ps. ix. 18) "The needy shall not alway be forgotten, [nor] the expectation of the poor shall perish for ever."

CONFUSIONS OF IDIOM

Christ forbade the Apostles to take anything at all for their journey. The Hebrew original would not lend itself to this corruption. But these precepts—as we might naturally suppose, and as we may infer from a reference to one of them in the First Epistle to Timothy[1]—must have been early appealed to in the Greek Churches, and, as being handed down through Greek oral tradition, must have been peculiarly liable to Greek corruption. Moreover, in a Greek-written Gospel the change of "except" to "not" would involve merely the dropping of one letter.[2]

This course has been adopted by Matthew and Luke. But why has Matthew omitted "bread," and altered "take" into "obtain"?

[267] (iii.) The reason probably is that Matthew, when editing, and throwing into the *second* person, the original tradition expressed in the *third* person, "that they should take no staff, *bread*," confused "bread" with the almost identical "*for themselves*," as appears to have been done once in Nehemiah.[3] This induces him not only to omit "bread," but also to introduce a verb in the middle voice, "obtain," meaning "procure for yourselves."

---

[1] 1 Tim. v. 18; comp. 1 Cor. ix. 13.

[2] [266*a*] "Except," in illiterate Greek = ιΜΗ. "Not" = ΜΗ. The dropping of ι would be facilitated by its coming after οΛō (*i.e.* οΛοΝ); οΛōι might be taken as an error for οΛοΝ. (Still more easily might ι be dropped after ΑιΡωcῑ).

In Lk. x. 4-5 ("Do not carry . . . and salute none by the way. But whatever house ye enter)" very slight changes indeed would restore the meaning, "Do not carry . . . anything on your journey. But salute whatever house ye enter," . . . μηδὲν(α) κατὰ τὴν ὁδόν. Ἀσπάσα(for η)σθε δ' εἰς ἣν ἂν εἰσέλθητε οἰκίαν. Codex D has εἰς ἣν ἂν δὲ . . .

The kind of Greek that might be expected in the earliest Greek Gospels may be illustrated by Böckh, *Gr. Inscr.* 4588, ι δαρα κε δι, *i.e.* εἰ δ' ἄρα καὶ δεῖ. It would probably be more similar to the Greek of the Apocalypse than to that of St. Paul's Epistles.

[3] Neh. v. 14, "*the bread of* (לחם) the governor," βίαν αὐτῶν, where αὐτῶν seems = "belonging to them" = להם, confused with לחם : βία = "governor," as also in next verse.

§ 16. "*In the Name because ye are Christ's*"

Mark ix. 41	Matth. x. 42
"For whoso shall give you to drink a cup of water *in the Name* because ye are Christ's."	"And whosoever shall give one of these little ones a cup of cold [water] *in* (lit. *to*) the name of a disciple."

[268] We are here confronted, in Mark, with a phenomenon unique in the Synoptic Gospels—Jesus calling Himself Christ, and that, too, not in the course of a special revelation to the disciples, but as (so to speak) a parenthetic assumption in the midst of discourse about other matters. Consequently, there is an antecedent probability that "because ye are Christ's" is an error arising from some original obscurity.

[269] The Jewish fathers use "the *Name*" absolutely for "the Name that is above every other name," that is, "the Name of God," as in the saying, "Noisome beasts come into the world for vain swearing and for profanation of the *Name*."[1]

[270] Jesus has previously said, "Whoso shall receive one such child *in* (lit. *on*) *my name* receiveth me, and whoso receiveth me receiveth him that sent me."[2] This implies that whosoever receives a "little one" in the name of the Father receives the Father Himself. The sense here, then, seems to require either "in *the* Name" or "in *my* name." Some authorities read in Mark "in *my* name"; but, if that was the original, why was it altered, since it makes excellent sense? It seems probable that the Hebrew original was "in the Name," meaning "in the Name of the Father in heaven," and that this caused a difficulty to all the evangelists.

[271] Luke has omitted the whole passage. Matthew

---

[1] Taylor's *Jewish Fathers*, v. 14, also iv. 7.
[2] Mk. ix. 37 (and simil. Mt. xviii. 5 and Lk. ix. 48).

appears to have identified "in the Name" with "to the name, credit, or account of," *i.e.* "for the sake of," or "as being." He inserts a passage about receiving a prophet, or righteous man, "for the sake of," or "as being," a prophet or righteous man; and then he seems to have conformed the original of Mark to this new context by inserting the words "of a disciple."

[272] Mark appears to have followed the practice of very early Christian writers in referring "the Name" to the Son who, as the Epistle to the Philippians says, has received "the Name that is above every name." The third Johannine Epistle says of certain faithful disciples that "for the sake of *the Name* they went forth," and similarly the Acts, "rejoicing that they were counted worthy to suffer dishonour for *the Name*." But in both passages the absence of a pronoun has caused the scribes difficulty; and so many manuscripts have inserted one that the Authorised Version gives on both occasions "*his* name."[1] But Mark, instead of inserting a pronoun, has inserted a marginal interpretation, "because ye are Christ's disciples," conflating it with "in the Name." This explains the otherwise inexplicable fact that in this single passage of the Synoptic Gospels Jesus appears to use the word "Christ" about Himself.

§ 17. *Hebraic Alternatives*

[272 (i)] We will conclude with an instance shewing that a Synoptic passage may contain manifest signs of error through mistranslation, but the phenomena may admit of more than one explanation.

Matth. xiii. 17	Luke x. 24
"Many prophets *and*	"Many prophets and *kings*

---

[1] [272*a*] The same interpolating tendency is apparent in many passages of Clem. Rom., Hermas, and Ignatius, *e.g.* Ign. *Eph.* 3, "For though I am a prisoner *in the Name*," where see Lightfoot's note.

CONFUSIONS OF IDIOM [272 (i)]

righteous [*men*] have passion-ately-desired to see the things on which ye-look."

have desired to see the things on which ye (emph.) look."

Of how many " kings " could Jesus say this ? Is there anything in Christ's doctrine, or in the special goodness of the kings of Israel or Judah, that would lead us to suppose that He would use language so favourable to royalty ?

(*a*) (?) " Princes."

Professor Resch suggests that the original had "princely" or "noble," a word translated by the LXX once " righteous," and twice "king".[1] But if that was the original, why did Luke give it the rare rendering " king "—contradicting all history too—when he might have rendered it " noble " ?[2] Moreover in Matthew elsewhere ("Ye build the sepulchres of the *prophets* and garnish the tombs of the *righteous*") where it is impossible to alter "righteous" into "kings," why does Luke omit the clause containing the word? And again, when Matthew distinguishes between " receiving a *prophet* " and " receiving a *righteous man* "—where once more " king " would be an impossible substitute—why does Luke omit the whole passage ? "[3]

(*b*) (?) " *Messengers of God.*"

These considerations make it necessary to consider an

---

[1] *Paralleltexte zu Lucas*, Leipsic, 1895. Prov. xvii. 7 "a prince," (נָדִיב) δικαίῳ, Prov. xix. 6 and Numb. xxi. 18 βασιλέων : נָדִיב = (11) ἄρχων, (3) εὐσεβής, (2) πρόθυμος, etc. : its radical meaning is "generous." Many may be so familiar with the sonorous words "prophets and kings," and perhaps with Mr. Maurice's book bearing this title—that they may feel as unwilling as the author felt at first to give up Luke's version. But let any reader dispassionately consider (i) how "many" of the Kings of Judah and Israel can be called decently "good," not to say rivals of prophets, (ii) how far from favourable to the general character of royalty are Christ's remarks about (Mk. x. 42) "those who are reputed to rule over the nations." Then surely it must seem impossible that He should have bestowed this eulogium on kings.

[2] Εὐγενής only occurs once in Heb. LXX, but Lk. has it twice Lk. xix. 12, Acts xvii. 11 : and it would have well expressed the double meaning of the Hebrew "princely."

[3] Mt. xxiii. 29 (Lk. xi. 47), Mt. x. 41.

alternative. Possibly the original, in all these passages of Matthew, as in a passage of Chronicles, coupled together "prophets" and "messengers of God." The latter term was applicable to Noah, Abraham, and many others, whom the Epistle to the Hebrews describes as having seen and greeted the promises "*from afar*." Jesus Himself says concerning the Baptist that he is "greater than a *prophet*," because he is the "*messenger*" predicted by Malachi.[1] Matthew — who occasionally (**162**) shows a tendency to paraphrase—may have habitually paraphrased "messengers of God," as "righteous persons." But it has been shown above (**105**) that "messenger" or "angel" (מלאך) is frequently confused with "king" (מלך) and was thus confused by the Chronicler in the story of Araunah. Luke appears to have been misled here by this confusion. In other passages where "king" is an impossible rendering, he omits the word and its context.[2]

The second (*b*) of these alternatives appears the more probable. But the first (*a*) is preferable to the view that Jesus coupled "kings" with "prophets," while tacitly excluding Noah, Abraham, Isaac, Moses, and all the rest (David alone excepted) of the "great cloud of witnesses."[3]

---

[1] 2 Chr. xxxvi. 16, Mt. xi. 9, Mal. iii. 1, "messenger": comp. Hag. i. 13, "the Lord's *messenger* (*i.e.* the prophet Haggai) in the Lord's message," ἄγγελος Κυρίου ἐν ἀγγέλοις Κυρίου.

[2] It is, however, possible that "prophets and righteous," wherever the phrase occurs, may be a conflation from *one original phrase*, "messengers of God." This might be interpreted by some as simply "prophets"—the reading of Syr. Cur. in Lk. x. 24 and in Tertull. *adv. Marc.* iv. 25 (quoted by Resch, *ad. loc.*)—by others (Euseb. *H.E.* x. 1. 4) conflated as "*righteous and witnesses of God.*" Since "messengers" = "angels," this might give rise to the Petrine tradition, which after saying (1 Pet. i. 10) "the *prophets* sought and searched diligently," adds (i. 12) "which things *the angels* desire to look into." And Mt.'s saying about "receiving a *righteous man*" may be another form of the tradition about (Heb. xiii. 2) "entertaining *angels* unawares." If the original was "messengers of God," Luke may have conflated the interpretation "prophets" with an alternative "kings" taken from the margin.   [3] Heb. xii. 1.

§ 18. *Conclusion*

[272 (ii)] The preceding pages make no attempt to answer questions as to the length of time necessary to produce our present Synoptic Gospels out of a combination of (i) written Hebrew Logia, (ii) various written interpretations of them in Aramaic and Greek, (iii) oral tradition in Aramaic and Hebrew : nor do they aim at analysing the Gospels into their (supposed) constituent parts, and assigning to each part its due authority. Interesting and important though these questions are, they must wait for their answer till students have agreed on what may seem to the general reader the comparatively uninteresting question discussed in this work : " Has, or has not, mistranslation been at work, producing divergences in the Gospels ? " It would be easy to show, for example, that *five years* have sufficed to produce marvellous differences in apparently honest writers, recording the life and death of Becket.[1] But such discussions, though they might apparently lead us swiftly and straight to fairly probable conclusions, would in the end be found to be very circuitous, or possibly to take us backward instead of forward. Internal evidence is a very slow guide, but a much safer one.

It is believed by the author that an amount of internal evidence has been brought before the reader to make it probable in some passages, highly probable in others, and almost certain in a few, that Synoptic discrepancies sprang from Hebrew mistranslated into Greek, and that the total result demonstrates that the Synoptic Gospels are in parts based on a Hebrew original. Nothing in this demonstration has been made to depend upon a theory as to the priority of this or that Gospel : but the conviction that Mark contains the Greek tradition from which (when slightly

[1] *St. Thomas of Canterbury, His Death and Miracles*, par. 838, A. and C. Black, 1898.

corrected) Matthew and Luke have borrowed, has been allowed weight so far as this, that Mark's text has been printed before the other two, and has been taken, hypothetically, as the earliest of the three Greek renderings.

Part II. of this series will aim at demonstrating the truth of this conviction. But it will also incidentally bring forward a great many more instances of Synoptic discrepancy explained by mistranslation.

THE END

www.ingramcontent.com/pod-product-compliance
Lightning Source LLC
Chambersburg PA
CBHW070917180426
43192CB00038B/1737